Come as You Are

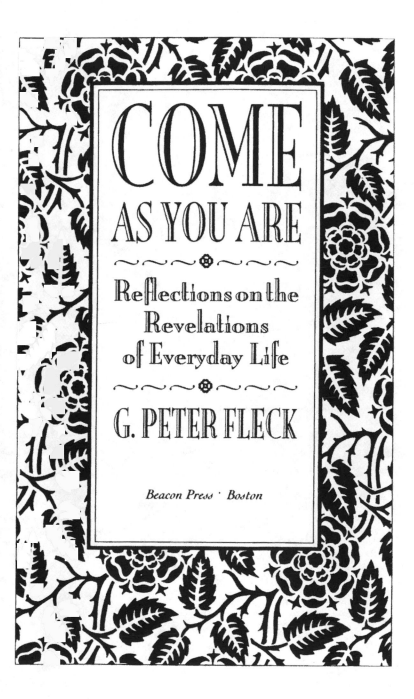

COME

AS YOU ARE

~~~ ❖ ~~~

Reflections on the
Revelations
of Everyday Life

~~~ ❖ ~~~

G. PETER FLECK

Beacon Press · Boston

Beacon Press
25 Beacon Street
Boston, Massachusetts 02108-2892
www.beacon.org

Beacon Press books
are published under the auspices of
the Unitarian Universalist Association of Congregations.

First digital-print edition 2001

Excerpt from *A Child's Christmas in Wales,* by Dylan Thomas, copyright © 1954 by New
Directions Publishing corp., reprinted by permission of New Directions and David Higham
Associates Ltd.; excerpt from *When We Were Very Young,* by A. A. Milne, copyright © 1924
by E. P. Dutton, renewed 1952 by A. A. Milne, reprinted by permission of Penguin USA and
Methuen Children's Books; excerpt from "The Road Not Taken," by Robert Frost, from *The
Poetry of Robert Frost,* edited by Edward Connery Lathem, copyright © 1916, 1969 by Henry
Holt and Company, Inc., copyright © 1944 by Robert Frost; reprinted by permission of Henr
Holt and Company, Inc., and Jonathan Cape Ltd.

Library of Congress Cataloging-in-Publication Data
Fleck, G. Peter.
Come as you are : reflections on the revelations of everyday life / G. Peter Fleck.
p.   cm.
ISBN 0-8070-1613-6
1. Meditations. 2. Spiritual life—Unitarian Universalist authors. 3. Fleck, G. Peter. I. Title.
BV4832.2.F587   1993
242—dc20   93-14978

To
Rachel,
Peter,
Benjamin,
Mary,
Jeremy,
Lauren,
and their
grandmother,
Ruth
Melchior
Fleck

Contents

III

LOVE

Acknowledgments

I express my deep appreciation to Wendy Strothman, director of Beacon Press, for her constructive criticism, which helped give this book its final form, and to Susan Worst for being available at all times to answer my most outrageous questions.

I express my grateful admiration to Missy Daniel, who edited the manuscript with extraordinary creativity and thoughtfulness, and to Chris Kochansky, who copyedited the manuscript with great expertise and understanding.

I am indebted to my dear friend and colleague The Reverend Kim Crawford Harvie for her editorial comments and suggestions.

I want to thank Jeannette Hopkins for her generous encouragement in the early stages of the book.

I'm grateful to Jan Maarten Boll, Esq., and Carla Josephus Jitta for their perceptive assistance in researching certain aspects of the so-called camp syndrome in the aftermath of the Nazi occupation of Holland, to Professor Dr. Ernst H. van der Beugel, who was kind enough to verify certain historical facts, and to Dr. Max Kohnstamm for his valuable suggestions.

Margaret Gilmore once again demonstrated her great competence and generosity in typing the manuscript.

As far as my wife Ruth's support is concerned, this book could not have been written without it.

I

FAITH

~1~

Don't Fret the Little Stuff

"Don't fret the little stuff." The meaning is clear; the grammar is wrong. It can be remedied by inserting one word: Don't fret *about* the little stuff. But straightening out the grammar blunts the meaning. So I say give me the wrong grammar with the unblunted meaning, which is: do not fret unless it is worthwhile. Do not let little things disturb you.

When our oldest daughter, Ann, now an associate professor at Simmons College School of Social Work, was six years old, she came home one day from school and told her mother of a disagreement with her classmates, the nature of which I don't remember. She expressed her feelings in the following post-script to her usual evening prayer:

> . . . and, please God, give that I may stick up for myself, and not to believe that I am wrong when I am right, and not to be disturbed unless it is very, very important.

There it is. Don't fret the little stuff. Don't fret unless it is very, very important.

Some people carry this thought one step further—they don't want to fret under any condition. One of the closest friends I ever had, a Unitarian minister long dead, used to admonish his congregation, "Let nothing steal away your peace of mind." I think he was wrong, because the ability to fret, to worry, to be disturbed, is essential to our humanity. It is the disturbance of our peace of mind that brings forth compassion and the desire to serve. Not to feel disturbed when one sees the dismal pictures of hungry children in our welfare hotels, not to be upset when a young person is killed, not to be shocked when two African-American boys are beaten up and one driven to his death in a near-lynching in Howard Beach, with the silent approval of the majority of the white population of that town, would be to re-nounce our involvement with the world for a mindless serenity. It would destroy our humanity. But so would the opposite: to permit little stuff to worry us, to hassle us, to steal away our peace of mind. Yet that is what we do so often. There almost seems to be some kind of law that keeps us fretting when there is nothing important to fret about, that makes us fret the little stuff.

There *is* such a law. Cyril Northcote Parkinson, a British author, historian, and journalist, formulated "Parkinson's Law" in a 1958 study of business administration. It holds that "work expands so as to fill the time available for its completion." Let's suppose that a certain job can be done in forty-five minutes. If one hour is allotted for that job, it will take that full hour, with no time to spare. How come? Well, the worker may reduce his speed. Or she may check a calculation that before remained unchecked, or write an explanatory introduction — you name it. We may apply Parkinson's Law to our fretting habits: if we have no major stuff that justifies fretting about, then we will fret the little stuff.

The Germans have a saying, "Worries are like fish — the big ones eat the small ones." We all have had that experience. I remember the days following the Nazi invasion of the Nether-lands. The experience was devastating, the implications apoca-lyptic. During those early days, the waiting rooms of the coun-try's psychiatrists and psychologists were empty. Total catastrophe had displaced preoccupation with neurotic problems. Displaced, mind you, *not* resolved. For the time being the overwhelming importance of the invasion had rendered lesser stuff unimportant. The importance of problems is relative.

Our grandson Peter wrote an illustration of this relativity in a college application essay:

> I had just finished playing an evening football game in a town about thirty miles from my home, and we had lost. As we trudged by the other team, I saw their elation and pride. Their smug smiles offended me as I left the dark stadium.
>
> Our bus ride was painfully prolonged by the coach's recriminations. He said we had given up. To escape my growing feelings of melancholy and self-pity, I turned and watched the factories and bars drift by. A station wagon pulled up alongside the bus. As we waited for the light to change, I noticed the little boy in the back of the Chevrolet. He was five or six, with soft, straight hair. He wore a dark blue sweatshirt, and he sat in a baby's carseat even though he looked a little old for it. We looked at one another. He smiled, and held up his thumb. In his eyes, apparently, we had won. I suddenly realized his eyes were puffy and slightly angled. He was a child with Down's Syndrome.
>
> His smile was beautiful, and I was touched by it. I thought about myself, my friends, my world, and I realized the embarrassing truth. We have grown accustomed to so much that we are easily distressed, while others with much greater problems remain cheerful. I waved back to the small boy and smiled a little. He grinned, and waved. All of a sudden, the fact that we had lost a football game seemed less important. What mattered was the boy in the station wagon. If the little boy saw me as a hero, I saw him as one too. And when the stoplight changed, we both were smiling.

No absolute criteria exist that can determine what is worth fretting about and what is not. All of us worry about sickness and death, about love relationships that break up, jobs that are lost, financial security that eludes us, unfulfilled ambitions, lost opportunities, things we did and shouldn't have done, things we should have done that remained undone. Paul's words from his letter to the Romans come to mind: "I do not do the good I want, but the evil I do not want is what I do." He must have fretted about it a great deal. These things are the *big* stuff.

Maybe the question of the relative bigness or littleness of the stuff is the wrong question. Maybe we should lower the threshold between the state of involvement *in* this world, with all the fretting it implies, and the state of detachment *from* this world, with the peace of mind *it* implies. Better still, maybe the two can be merged. Maybe it is possible to confront what disturbs us in this world with the peace of mind achieved by those who detached themselves from this world. This may be what my old friend had in mind with his charge "Let nothing steal away your peace of mind."

In the story of Mary and Martha in Luke's Gospel, Jesus admonishes Martha for being "anxious and troubled about many things," and tells her, rather, that only "one thing is needful." Most of us are like Martha. The manifold small things that trouble our hearts reflect our over-commitment to the world. If we serve too many causes, if we want to right too many wrongs, if we want to be the perfect partner, spouse, friend, host, or neighbor, if we feel responsible for everything and everybody, then we will become unable to take responsibility for anybody or anything. That is the essence of Jesus's warning to Martha, who is anxious about many small things.

There are things that seem to justify our being troubled by them. The sickness and death of someone close to us, the end of a love relationship, the loss of a job, a financial crisis — these seem to justify our anxiety. But that is not what Jesus says. He says not to be troubled by anything except one thing, the thing Mary is concerned about when she sits at his feet and listens to his teaching.

Jesus admonished his disciples, saying, "In me you may have peace. In the world you have tribulation; but be of good cheer, I have overcome the world." And again: "Peace I leave with you; my peace I give to you; . . . let not your hearts be troubled, neither let them be afraid." And,

> "Do not be anxious, saying, 'What shall we eat?' or 'What shall we drink?' or 'What shall we wear?' . . . But seek first his kingdom and its righteousness, and all these things shall be yours as well. Take therefore no thought for the morrow, for the morrow shall take thought for the things of itself. Sufficient unto the day is the sorrow thereof."

It all adds up to this admonition: Don't worry. Have faith, faith that in the end all will be well.

The Mahayana branch of Buddhism expresses a similar ideal in the concept of the Bodhisattva, one who, having gained enlightenment—that is, being ready for Nirvana—chooses to return to the world to help other beings toward *their* release, confronting the disturbances of the world with peace of mind derived from their own enlightenment. Most of us have not reached that stage of enlightenment; most of us do not have that peace of mind, at least not all the time. But we try. The first step is to dismiss from our minds the little stuff and to fret only when it is very, very important.

~2~

The Road Not Taken

Two roads diverged in a wood, and I —
I took the one less traveled by,
And that has made all the difference.
ROBERT FROST, *"The Road Not Taken"*

The moral is clear, though not spelled out. Having taken the less-traveled road, the traveler found that it enriched his life. Decisively. It turned out to make all the difference.

There is another implication: in choosing one road, the traveler gives up the other. He regrets — being one traveler — that he cannot follow both roads. He comforts himself by saying, "I kept the first for another day." But he doubts he will ever come back. And so do we. The road not taken, the missed opportunity, never comes back. We will never walk that road. We will never know its mysteries.

When I was twenty-two, I drove my Ford convertible from Amsterdam to the Italian province of Tuscany for a two-week vacation. The beauty of Tuscany — its countryside, its Renaissance cities, its Romanesque and Gothic churches, its art treasures — was all breathtaking. I was struck powerfully by the evidence of a symbiosis of humans and nature that had existed for uncounted generations. Many vineyards that still produce were there in the heyday of the Roman Empire. One day, toward the end of my vacation, I passed a sign that read, "Rome 180 Kilometers." One hundred and eighty kilometers is a hundred and twenty miles. A two- to three-hour drive. I had only two, maybe two and a half, days left to see Rome. I stopped at the roadside to think it through. I thought of the great painters and poets of Northern Europe who went to live in Rome for an extended period, sometimes for a year or more, to experience its powerful beauty and to be inspired by the majesty of its history. To "do" Rome in two days seemed a barbarian insult to all Rome stood for. I decided not to take that road. And I am here to testify that I have never been to Rome.

After my high school years, when I lived abroad in the late twenties, I spent several summer vacations traveling as a passenger on freight boats destined for places that in those pre-Hilton days were well off the beaten path. On one of those trips, which originated in Le Havre, the boat was to dock at Algiers for one day, and I was thrilled by the prospect of setting foot on the "dark continent."

I was so fascinated by the beauty of the city and the mysteries of the "Casbah" that I let the boat leave without me. After a few days I decided to travel south into the desert. I got on a bus that crossed the Atlas mountains and somehow arrived in the oasis village of Bou Saada. There I met a young Arab guide and for many days we rode on horseback into the desert, visiting other desert villages. I was captivated by a sense of timelessness never before experienced; nothing, it seemed to me, had changed since biblical days.

My companion had to fast during the day; it was the end of Ramadan. He explained how its observance relates to life eternal and described the Arab heaven, which awaits the believer with its gold-paved streets, in the literal existence of which he firmly believed.

Wherever we were, he would say his prayers three times a day. But he was eager to point out that if you were physically handicapped you were excused from prostrating yourself, if you were sick in bed it would suffice to bow your head, and if you were too weak to do that, it was sufficient to close your eyes. "Comme ça, vous voyez?"

The days passed and I don't think I ever felt more content. The fact that my parents had no idea where I was lent a rather pleasing pungency to my bliss.

Then one day we came across a tombstone sticking out of the sand a few miles from the village. We stopped to read the inscription. It was the grave of a Swede who as a young man had come to Bou Saada for a short visit and had stayed on.

I decided that it was time for me to take the road home.

Many years later, in January of 1953, I was invited to preach in Plainfield, New Jersey, on "Layman's Sunday." It affected me in a way I had not expected. I had spoken in public on enough occasions to not be overly fearful about confronting an audience. Of course I was nervous. (I still am every time I go into the pulpit; I think one has to be.) Of course I was relieved when all went well. But the surprise was the feeling of joyful exultation I experienced in sharing with the congregation thoughts on ultimate things, things that dealt with basic religious questions.

On this occasion I experienced for the first time that one preaches God's word—and not one's own. In the pulpit you are a conduit for something that is beyond you. You are an intermediary and not a principal, an instrument for something greater than yourself. Indeed, in conducting a worship service you are a minister, literally a servant. What is being done is being done through you, not by you.

One thing became clear to me on that Sunday and it has made all the difference since: I wanted to preach. But the question was, Where and to whom? I shared my thoughts with the minister, our dear friend H. Mortimer Gesner, Jr. Mort was warmly supportive. To say that he taught me homiletics would be using a big word in vain. But he did take me more than once into the empty sanctuary and let me read all kinds of texts from the pulpit, seating himself alternately in the front pew and the back pew, telling me to slow down, to speak more articulately, not to lower my voice at the end of a sentence, in order to be heard, heard, heard, all over the sanctuary.

It was a full year before I had an opportunity to preach again. Mort had invited a young minister to preach in Plainfield and had undertaken to supply a substitute to fill the guest preacher's own pulpit, in Point Lookout, at the easternmost tip of Long Island. And so it came to pass that Ruth and I set out one snowy Saturday afternoon in January on the road that led to the far end of Long Island. We spent a spooky night as the only guests in a huge hotel. It was closed for the winter, but the janitor was found willing to rent us a room. (I suspected this was for his personal financial benefit, but he might have liked putting us up anyway, for, as he told us, he had "not seen a soul for many days"—a remark that did not contribute to our peace of mind.)

The service in Point Lookout went well and the experience strengthened my strange urge to preach. Mort spoke to the Unitarian regional director and met with a cool reception. The thought of putting laypeople in the pulpit did not appeal to him, understandably so. But he did take my telephone number and, miracle of miracles, he called me in April because the minister of the Unitarian church in Trenton was looking for a replacement on the last Sunday of the month. Then came Rutherford and Orange and Princeton and Bethlehem, Pennsylvania. This was the beginning of the process that led to my ordination in 1984.

Frost's poem suggests that the choices we make in our lives are vitally important. When we choose one road we reject all others, and that is the way it is. We can only choose one road at a time, and when we do so many other choices seem to fall by the wayside. Similar choices may present themselves later on, but they will only be similar choices, never the same choices.

I am a missed-opportunity person. I mourn the opportunities that life offered me and that I did not take because other duties and responsibilities called. Missed opportunities are, indeed, the most painful implication of the road not taken. But there is one road I took almost forty years ago, the road to a church in Point Lookout. For me that was the road less traveled by, and it *has* made all the difference.

~3~

Accepting One's Fate

"What are you preaching on this Sunday?" Ruth asked recently. "On accepting one's fate," I said. "It seems to me that there is not much else you can do with your fate but accept it," she replied. And I realized that if I adopted her line of thought it would be a very short sermon. But it is not that simple. There is an alternative to accepting one's fate—quarreling with it.

Fate is that which befalls us. It is our fortune, our lot, our destiny.

The word *fate* does not occur in the Bible. In the Jewish and Christian traditions there was no room for the concept of fate as an independent power. The will of God determined human destiny. Jesus accepted his fate with the words "Not as I will but as thou wilt." Before him, Job had accepted the tragedies that befell him with these words: "The Lord gave, and the Lord has taken away; Blessed be the name of the Lord."

The concept of fate as an independent power derives from the Greek tradition. The ancient Greeks did not believe in an all-powerful God whose will determined human fate. Zeus, senior among many gods and goddesses, was like a chairman of the board of a large corporation, powerful but far from all-powerful. Three goddesses, the Fates, or *Parcae,* formed a kind of troika to preside over the birth and life and death of every human being. Were they carrying out preexisting plans? Did they follow instructions from a higher power, or did they act randomly on the spur of the moment? Greek mythology does not answer these questions, but it is clear that each human being's life and death was determined irrevocably, unalterably, inevitably. Men and women were puppets, acting out a script they had not written.

In the Greek legend it was prophesied that Oedipus would kill his father and marry his mother. To avert this destiny, his parents gave Oedipus, at his birth, to a servant whom they ordered to abandon the infant to die in the wilderness. Oedipus was discovered by a shepherd of the local king, who brought him up in his palace as his own son. Whereupon Oedipus's fate proceeded to take its terrible course.

Jesus and Job accepted their fate by accepting God's will. In the Greek tradition there was no such acceptance. When they realized what they had done, Oedipus's mother hanged herself and Oedipus blinded himself and went into solitary exile. They turned against themselves because they had no alternative. Some of us still take things out on ourselves; many suicides are provoked by the inability of individuals to accept their fate.

But it is often hard for us to accept our fate. We imagine that we deserve better. Our fate, however, is not determined by our merits or demerits. It is not tit for tat. Job's fate resulted from God's frivolous wager with Satan, an unlikely story invented to explain why the just suffer and the unjust prosper so often. This remains one of the deep, unanswered religious questions.

To accept our fate or to quarrel with it? At times we do both. At times we know how good life can be, at times we know how cruel it can be. The premature death of a young person is among our most devastating experiences. It may be caused by a car accident, by AIDS, by a brain tumor; the possibilities abound.

As we grow older, death, always in the back of our mind, moves to the forefront. It has its own blessings, its own rewards, and sometimes brings the discovery of unsuspected reserves of strength, spirituality, creativity, and love. Yet it does not lose its terrible sadness. One still learns many things.

I have often learned from my grandchildren. Our youngest grandson, Jeremy, was born with some learning disabilities, visual difficulties, and problems with motor skills, all due to fetal stress during his delivery. He went through years of physical therapy. One day when he was five, his mother apologized to him for all the trouble he had to go through. But he interrupted her, saying, "That's all right, Mom. Everyone has handicaps. I just know mine better than others know theirs."

In the spring of 1990, Ruth and I attended the inaugural meeting of the Brain Tumor Society, which is dedicated to the support of brain tumor patients and their families and to raising money for research. There were four hundred guests, including the leading medical experts in the field. All those present were in one way or another connected with the dreaded disease, either because they themselves suffered from it or because a loved one did. We attended because our oldest grandchild, Rachel, was the keynote speaker. She was twenty-two years old. One year earlier she had been diagnosed with an inoperable brain tumor. Rachel's courage, her fighting spirit, her resolve to live and be well remind one of others who also lead radiantly creative lives against great odds. By their spiritual strength they enrich the lives of all of us. Like Seth Feldman, who died of a brain tumor after his ardent wish to be admitted to the college of his choice had been fulfilled. He lived to the end of the first semester. The vibrancy of his life and its joyfulness inspired his friends to honor Seth's memory by organizing Campuses Against Cancer, a rapidly growing organization that raises funds for brain tumor research.

Things happen during our earthly lives that we can neither bring about nor avoid. We succumb to illness. We die prematurely. An otherwise healthy child is born without a right hand.

Some children are dyslexic. Careers and marriages crumble. Countless things happen to all of us, good things and bad things that together constitute our fate.

At times most of us quarrel with our fate: If only I had not been born without a right hand. If only I were better looking. If only I were more intelligent, more successful, more assertive, less bashful. If only my parents had been more encouraging, more loving. But this quarreling with our fate is a loss of time, a loss of energy, a loss of happiness. It is senseless, because our fate is a given. Fate is not subject to negotiation, change, or compromise. Its "givenness" is total.

But that is only half the story. For the total "givenness" of our fate is matched by the total freedom we have to react to our fate as we choose. It is as if we were dealt a hand of cards. Whether the cards we are dealt are preordained to be ours or randomly distributed makes no difference. Either way we have no influence on the cards we receive. But once we have them in our hand we are free to play them as we choose.

We celebrate that freedom. It may well be what life is all about. It may well be our highest calling.

~4~

Lines and Squares

In the poem "Lines and Squares," by A. A. Milne, Christopher Robin creates his own phobias. If he steps on a line that separates the squares with which some London streets are paved, he will be devoured by the bears

> Who wait at the corners all ready to eat
> The sillies who tread on the lines of the street.

The same process that creates the phobia creates its cure, because if he keeps in the squares, "the masses of bears . . . go back to their lairs."

In Christopher Robin's magic world of little boys and big bears the ultimate control is left with Christopher Robin himself. As long as he steps on the squares and not on the lines—and that is in his power—he is safe. So he triumphantly calls out,

> "Bears,
> Just watch me walking in all the squares!"

Christopher Robin feels secure. He is not yet aware of the mind's ambiguities. He does not understand the attractiveness, yes, the seductiveness, that causes people to bring about the very catastrophe they want to avoid.

All of us stand with one foot in Christopher Robin's magic world. His particular obsession is so widespread that it found its way into the jingle "Step on a crack, break your mother's back." Here the magic thinker does not threaten himself but takes it out on his mother. We find a similar transference in the magical thinking of "primitive" tribes who put pins or nails in dolls representing their enemies, believing they can harm them by doing so.

We are neither like Christopher Robin, who after all is a little boy, nor like the tribesman, yet all of us — erudite as we may be and mature as we may seem — indulge in magical thinking. We may not pour water on the ground to bring about rain, but we do say "touch wood" to avert bad luck. (The wood in this expression, incidentally, is supposed to be the wood of the cross.)

Our oldest daughter, Ann, tells the story of a bad plane trip she took when she was thirteen or fourteen. She was afraid and kept watching one of the engines from her window seat, as if her watching the engine would reduce, if not eliminate, the danger of malfunction. When lunch was served she did not eat. Whereupon her neighbor, a middle-aged gentleman who had finished his lunch, said to her, "You can eat your lunch, kiddo. I'll watch the engine for you."

Our middle granddaughter, Mary, had similar fears when she was put on a plane for her first solo trip. Clutching her stuffed whale tightly, she said, "I am not scared, but my whale is."

Magic is not the same as superstition, though the demarcation line is not always clear. Still, I think one could say that superstition is the belief in things that are not true, while magical thinking is an effort to influence the course of events by one's thoughts and words.

Our middle daughter, Andrea, used to write a weekly column in the 1970s for the *Daily Tribune* in Ames, Iowa. In one column she wrote:

When I was five and about to acquire a sibling, my older sister (then six) and I understood with perfect clarity that we would be better off if the imminent baby was another girl. A son would be a phenomenon, a whole new show with which we could not possibly compete. Whereas a sister would be a manageable threat.

To effect our ardent wish, we would sit opposite each other, holding hands, and chant: "I hope it is a boy, I hope it is a boy," expressing our hope for the brother we feared. The eventual birth of a sister was a relief, but hardly a surprise.

Andrea claimed that "magic thinking wins converts and keeps the faithful primarily by humbling the braggart." She recalled an excursion with friends on a particularly cold evening when she chanced to say of their car, "It starts no matter how cold it is." "Knock it off," her husband muttered. "Really," she insisted. "It's a terrific cold weather car." "That's it," exploded her husband, who is a supposedly rational scientist. "Now you've jinxed us for sure. This car will never start tonight." But it did start and she was still hooting with glee when the gas line froze up, the engine died, and they sat in awful silence at 1:00 A.M. with the temperature at minus eighteen degrees. This, Andrea explained, was an extreme case; as a rule, even "the glimmer of a gloat, the merest suggestion of a brag, is sufficient to precipitate some manner of catastrophe."

Magic and superstition both bring into our lives elements of unreality and untruth. The bears will *not* devour you when you step on the line. Taking your eyes off the engine will *not* cause an accident. Saying "touch wood" will *not* avert disaster. Expressing preference for a little brother will *not* convert the unborn child into a little sister. Bragging will *not* bring about catastrophe.

Our religion demands that we emancipate ourselves from magic and superstition. I hear the atheist observe that "religion itself is nothing but superstition. You suggest that we drive out the devil with Beelzebub!" I don't deny that religion has, at times, been host to superstition and magic. Maybe the purification of religion from both of these is what liberal religion is all about. But in the process there is the danger of overdoing it, as in cleaning an old painting. First, the refinisher removes all the layers of dirt and varnish that have accumulated over the years. In the process the colors become more vivid, the design clearer. However, beyond a certain point the colors will become faint, and ultimately the bare canvas will show through.

In our eagerness to eliminate all magic and superstition from our religion we may forget that much in religion is not to be taken literally but metaphorically. The true is not necessarily factual, nor is the factual necessarily true. It has been said that we have a choice between taking our religion literally or taking it seriously. As Elie Wiesel once said, the truth is too complex for our human mind to fathom, "but let me tell you a story...." That story may not be factual, but it may nevertheless deal with the truth.

Christopher Robin's magic world of lines and squares is the very opposite of our religious world. In his world, stepping on the lines brings retribution. Sins are punished; the bears eat you. In our religion, no one eats us. Allowance is made for our imperfection. Sins can be forgiven. Jesus said to the woman who was taken in adultery, "Neither do I condemn you; go, and sin no more." We all live by the grace of these words.

~5~

Living with Grace

Augustine, that giant among the church fathers, once wrote, "What is Grace? I know until you ask me. When you ask me I [no longer] know."

I do not have the illusion that I am smarter than Saint Augustine; I cannot define grace either. Still, I can submit some of its attributes.

Grace is a blessing, a blessing that is undeserved, unsolicited, and unexpected, a blessing that brings a sense of the divine order of things into our lives. The ways of grace are mysterious, we cannot figure them out. But we know grace by its fruits, by the blessings of its works.

On the strength of what I have said so far, we would expect to be startled when grace manifests itself. The opposite is true. It doesn't startle us at all, for grace is everywhere. We may not discern it, we may not recognize it, for we are inclined to take it for granted, like breathing and the ongoing use we make of our senses.

I came across this satirical version of the Sermon on the Mount:

> Then Jesus took his disciples up the mountain and gathering them around him, he taught them, saying:

Blessed are the poor in spirit,
  for theirs is the kingdom of heaven.
Blessed are the meek.
Blessed are they that mourn.
Blessed are the merciful.
Blessed are they who thirst for justice.
Blessed are you who are persecuted.
Blessed are you when you suffer.
  Be glad and rejoice
    for great is your reward in heaven
      and remember what I am telling you.
Then Simon Peter said,
  "Do we have to write this down?" . . .
And James said,
  "Will we have a test on this?" . . .
And Bartholomew said,
  "Do we have to turn this in?"
And John said,
  "The other disciples didn't have to learn this." . . .
And Judas said,
  "What does this have to do with real life?"

Grace had gone unrecognized.

Another story makes this very point. A small church in a remote rural area had been without a minister for some time. When a new minister was assigned, it caused upheaval among the parishioners — especially among the men — for the new minister was a woman. She was dismayed and sought an opportunity to gain their confidence. She learned that on Saturdays some of the men were accustomed to go fishing on the lake. She asked if she might join them. They met at the agreed-upon hour and embarked in a rowboat. After some time, one of the men said, "We must go back — we left the bait on the beach." "Let *me* do it. I'll be back in no time," the minister said. She stepped out of the boat and began to walk toward the shore. The men were silent. Then one said, "Not only did they send us a woman, but they sent us one who can't even swim."

Grace moves in mysterious ways. Like many of us, I have done my share of flying on commercial airlines. Only once did I have the feeling that my life was endangered. Ordinarily I would have taken the shuttle from La Guardia to Boston, but shuttle service was suspended that evening because (as I learned later) crosswinds made landing in Boston hazardous. I was told that USAir, then a struggling newcomer among the airlines, would fly from Newark to Boston at 9:00 P.M. I got the last available seat. Grace, you might think. Don't jump to conclusions! We left Newark at 9:30, circled for half an hour over Boston, tried three times to land. By now it was well past 11:00. The captain addressed us over the public address system; he apologized for not being able to land, but he was pleased to report that we had sufficient fuel to resort to "Plan B." Being ignorant of the existence of "Plan A," I could only muster limited enthusiasm for "Plan B," and the mention of fuel and our dependence on it alarmed me. I remember that I thought, So this is what it feels like to be headed for disaster. But what do you *do* in a case like that? Nothing — there is nothing you *can* do. I wondered what the other passengers were thinking. They must have had similar thoughts. No one showed concern. The situation was too serious for panic. Finally we landed, on "the blessed soil of Hartford" (to quote Jean Kerr), and were transported by bus to Boston, arriving at 3:00 A.M.

Before leaving Newark I had phoned home. Throughout the long night Ruth was in touch with USAir. The information was ominous. Then at last came the jubilant news. "They landed in Hartford." Ruth said, *"Hart*ford, Con*nect*icut???" "Lady," said the operator, "you don't understand — they are on the ground." At that moment Ruth realized that we had landed by God's grace.

In 1941, a cousin of Ruth's, who was about to give birth, fled from Paris just before the Nazi occupation. She was able to reach a hospital in a small town in the south of France. There her boy was born. He was perfect except for his club feet. The local doctors told the mother that neither in their hospital nor in any known to them in that part of the country was there a surgeon able to perform the corrective operation, but they did know that it had to be performed within forty-eight hours after birth. Then a young nurse spoke up; she had heard that the famous Professor X, the great expert on this particular operation, had arrived in town yesterday, also on a flight from Paris to escape the Nazis. The town was small, the fame of the professor great, and he was found after a short search. He performed the operation that same evening. Grace, pure grace, in a world of disgrace.

Sometimes grace is recognized only in retrospect. For isn't it true that all of us have memories of moments in our lives when grace was manifest, when we were comforted, upheld, protected by grace? When strength was given to us beyond the strength we could muster, courage beyond the courage we had?

For Ruth and me, one central event in our lives exemplifies grace to us. It was our escape from Nazi-occupied Holland. To escape seemed impossible. Yet it became possible as a result of the concern of some people, their friendship, their ability to make things happen. Even so, the escape seemed to elude us until the very last moment.

The scheduled date of our departure came closer and closer. Before we could leave the country, however, one more document was required—a visa for Spain or Portugal, the only countries from which ships still sailed to the Western Hemisphere. The granting of such a visa, in turn, depended on the recipient having passage on one of those ships, and that was impossible to obtain because they were all booked up for many months in advance and the steamship companies no longer accepted deposits.

The Spanish Consulate was in The Hague. I had been to see

the consul twice. I had gained the impression that he wanted to be helpful, given a chance to accommodate me. I shared my impression with an elderly manager of an Amsterdam travel bureau, whom I vaguely knew. Together we developed the following plan. He would send a cable to the Spanish steamship company, reserving passage for Ruth and me on the SS *Magellanes* (this name was randomly picked out of a list of scheduled sailings), due to depart from the Spanish port of Bilbao on April 12. Before he could receive an answer, which was bound to be negative, he would write me a letter confirming that he had reserved passage for us on that ship and send a messenger to The Hague who would present to the Spanish consul a copy of his confirmation, together with our two passports, with the request to stamp the visas therein.

All this was planned in the early morning. Toward evening of that same day, a messenger of the travel bureau appeared on our doorstep with our passports in which the Spanish consul had stamped the visas. Grace, pure grace. Ten days later we arrived in Bilbao, after going through customs at the resort town of San Sebastian.

We arrived in San Sebastian late at night and, as far as I was concerned, with a fearful heart. For while we had Spanish visas, we did not have the steamship tickets on the strength of which the visas had supposedly been issued, and I realized that this could spell trouble. The basic rule governing the fate of refugees is, Don't let in what you can't get out.

After looking at our passports and at us, the immigration officer behind the desk asked for our tickets. I produced the confirmation letter from the Amsterdam travel agency written in English. He scrutinized it carefully. Did he know English or did he just pretend to? If he did, I don't think that he believed for one moment that our reservations were genuine. He looked at us again and let us pass without asking any further questions. Maybe it was a gesture of Spanish *grandezza*, the *noblesse oblige* attitude which, though threadbare, is still abroad in that country as a residue of its golden age, when the sun did not set on its empire.

The next morning, we paid the first of many daily visits to the ticket agency, where refugees from Germany and all Nazi-occupied countries queued up to get accommodations on their tickets, which the steamship companies had grossly oversold. Having no tickets at all, we realized that our stay in Bilbao might be an extended one.

Our memories of that stay, oddly enough, are happy ones. After the daily trip to the ticket agency, we used to go for walks in the surrounding hills, from which one invariably looked out on the Mediterranean, whose blueness turns, late in the day, to purple—Homer's "wine-coloured sea."

Food was scarce and consisted mainly of fish cooked in olive oil. I got some form of dysentery and went to see a doctor. He cured me but refused to be paid. Wasn't I a refugee? He never accepted money from refugees. He wished me luck. The only food available in some stores was fruit, oranges and bananas. Every morning we bought our daily supply in a little store run by a kind, round-faced old woman.

One day our routine visit to the ticket agency office brought us the solution of our problem: the Argentine ambassador to Spain—so we were told—had canceled a whole suite of cabins for himself, his wife, the children, and his retinue. We were offered a tiny cabin reserved for the ambassador's butler. We accepted gratefully. It was then that we were given the name of the ship and the date of its departure. It was the SS *Magellanes*, leaving on April 12—the very ship, the very date on which the Amsterdam travel bureau had made its original quasi-reservation. This coincidence was somehow comforting to us, and was itself a sign of grace. For it was through grace that a grotesque situation had somehow led to an orderly, legitimate end. (Several years after the war I learned that more than twenty other people were eventually able to escape in the same way we did.)

On the eve of our departure we went to say goodbye to the old round-faced woman who had sold us her bananas and oranges every morning. She asked us to wait, disappeared into the room behind the counter, and came back with a jar of home-made jam that she insisted we accept as a farewell gift, a farewell gift to us who were about to leave her famished land for the abundance of the United States. On April 12 the *Magellanes* sailed to Vigo, where more passengers and freight were taken on board, and from there we began the long westward journey away from the Nazi-ridden continent.

In the middle of the third night after leaving Vigo, I woke up. It was deadly silent. The throbbing sound of the ship's engines had stopped. We were either adrift or riding at anchor. Both were ominous, for I could only think of one explanation: the Nazis had at last invaded Spain and had called back our over-loaded refugee ship.

At sunrise we went on deck and were told that the ship's rudder had been damaged. It might be repairable at sea; if not we would have to return to Spain. It was not a convincing story, but when the captain appeared by noon, his confirmation lent credibility to it. Toward evening the ship turned around and at slow speed began to retrace its short journey, back to Spain.

The next two weeks we spent in drydock in Ferrol, a Spanish navy base situated on the western tip of Spain's north coast. For reasons of hygiene and limited food supply, the passengers were encouraged to leave the ship during the day and forage for themselves in the town, which turned out to be a rather unproductive enterprise.

We resumed our Bilbao-like walks in the hilly countryside, but with less gusto and on a more limited scale. The military activities in and around Ferrol may have made us more cautious in our movements; then, too, it may have been the discouragement of once again being caught, for an unknown period of time, in the very situation we had tried to escape. The days followed each other in anxious succession. After two weeks, the overcrowded *Magellanes* resumed her westward journey.

Don't ask me why God, who through grace could save the baby from growing up with club feet, did not prevent the child from being born with club feet in the first place. Don't ask me why Ruth and I were saved while millions perished. Why was grace not more even-handed? To raise the question may well be blasphemous. Not to raise it would be inhuman. So I raise it. But I cannot answer it.

Thus we are confronted once again with the great mystery into which we are born and of which we are a part. It raises many questions. I have a hunch that one day it may yield an answer.

And then again, it may not.

~6~

Surviving

I had a sister two and a half years my senior. When we were three and six years old, we were at the beach and stood on a sandcastle we had built in anticipation of the incoming tide. The water rose and soon surrounded us. It rose further and began to erode the base of our edifice. Standing on the sagging sand heap we chanted at the top of our voices:

> *We staan nog op ons berregje*
> *en niemand is nog nat.*
>
> We still stand on our mou—ountain,
> nobody is wet—yet.

Many years later, when the foundation of the world in which we grew up was sagging and came apart, we used the words *"we staan nog op ons berregje"* as a code for hanging in there, for having survived so far.

A sense of survival is deeply embedded in our genes. Our ancestors lived "in spite of," not "because of." They survived under conditions of marginality that would have extinguished them had they been less firmly established in their identity. Like some Alpine flowers, they sank their roots in the scant soil between the cracks and crevices of the rocks that formed their environment. There they bloomed and flourished until the rains and the wind dissipated the soil around their roots and washed them away to another similarly marginal habitat, or into oblivion.

Whatever generic sense of survival I was born with was nourished by the Dutch environment. For the Dutch are a nation of survivors, threatened as they have always been by the sea and by the military power and cultural influence of the large European nations that surround them. "Holland annexes itself," Bismarck is supposed to have said. He was wrong. Hitler may have thought that the supposed racial kinship between the Germans and the Dutch would perpetuate his hold over the country. The Dutch said no, and, infuriated, he ordered plans to be drawn for the deportation of the entire population and the resettling of the country by Germans.

A typical unpoetic Dutch saying proclaims, *"Wie niet sterk is moet slim wezen"* (Whoever lacks strength needs cunning). *"Luctor et emergo,"* which may be rendered freely as "I struggle and survive," is the motto under the coat of arms of the Dutch province of Zeeland, which shows a heraldic lion emerging from a stylized body of water. Through cunning and struggle the Dutch survived.

I was born a marginal, sick-looking child, according to my mother. My nurse, who adored me, used to bring my mother to tears by saying, "He is so pale, I wonder whether he will stay with us. He is too good for this world." I wasn't. I stayed, and I have never regretted it.

~7~

What Does the Turtle Rest On?

When I was in grade school—I may have been nine or ten or eleven years old—I learned that somewhere in India there is a Hindu tribe whose members believe that the earth and the sky above it rest on an elephant, and that the elephant stands on a turtle.

I remember that when I was told the story I was troubled by one particular aspect of it. It was not the role of the elephant. Maybe I had already heard of Atlas, to whom the Greeks imparted a similar role; if so, the analogy may have reassured me. Nor did I feel disturbed by the idea of this obviously mythical elephant resting on an equally mythical turtle. What did bother me, however, was that apparently nobody had raised the question And what does the turtle rest on? It was the absence of that question, let alone a satisfactory answer to it, that made me feel that our Western way of thinking was superior to what I experienced as the primitive ways of the East. But is it?

The Bible opens with the words "In the beginning God created . . ." But "Who created God?" is not a valid theological question. God forbid.

Paul Tillich speaks of "the God beyond God," that is, "the God who appears when God has disappeared in the anxiety of doubt." Somehow this seems to suggest that there is something,

31

after all, on which the turtle rests, though it's not clear what that is. Maybe it is a camel on which the turtle rests, comfortably snuggled between its humps, in which case it would behoove some German theologian to become lyrical and write a book about so much Wisdom in the Universe. For don't you see that if it were not a camel but, let's say, a whale, the turtle might easily slip off its back and the whole thing would come tumbling down? On the other hand, maybe it *is* a whale, for then the question What does the whale stand on? would not arise. Obviously the whale does not stand on anything, because it swims. Swims? In what? Well, in water—wet, splashy water, the ocean.

In theology there is a point beyond which no questions are asked. That point for most religious people is the turtle. Even if there is a "turtle beyond the turtle," regardless of whether it is a camel or a whale, that's it. That's where the theological buck stops.

Not so with science. Science never stops asking questions. A scientist once told me that valid answers to scientific problems should raise more questions than they answer. In which case science is in for a long haul.

The trouble with questions about causes, especially causes of behavior, is that the same cause will make different people behave in different ways. Why am I overweight? Because when I was a child there was never enough to eat. So I overcompensate and indulge. Why is my brother underweight? Because when he was a child there was never enough to eat. So he never learned to enjoy food and has guilt feelings when he eats.

The same cause leads to different results. What kind of a cause is that? A "non-cause" cause. What is the real cause? Is there possibly something in us in the end that determines the result of the "non-cause" cause?

The ancients believed in astrological causes, and so do an increasing number of our contemporaries. But even the Romans held that *"astra inclinant non cogunt"* (the stars influence but do not force), thus leaving at least some leeway for that "something in us." Shakespeare expressed this thought by having Cassius say to Brutus that the fault was not in the stars but "in ourselves."

Or is that "something in ourselves" possibly an illusion, and is there, beyond the stars, a force that inexorably predestines our fate? Is it possible that the cause within us and the stellar cause and the ultimate predestinating cause relate to each other as the elephant, the turtle, and the camel or the whale?

What if that ultimate predestinating cause turned out to be some chemical mysteriously embedded in our genes? Then the universe would again be turned into itself, like a drawing by M. C. Escher.

Causes, in the end, are not at all self-evident or easy to establish. Today I give the Hindu myth a different reading. For I have come to the conclusion that in the last analysis, whether it is science or philosophy or theology, there is always that ultimate turtle on whom everything rests and who, in turn, rests on nothing.

~8~

The Passage of Time

Today I will write about time and the way it passes. Time is not linear. These words state so obvious a truth that somebody must have said or written them before. Was it MacLuhan, Marcuse, or Aristotle? It makes no difference. But if not linear, what form or forms does time take? God only knows. Though even that is an open question. For someone in whose sight "a thousand years . . . are but as yesterday when it is past, or as a watch in the night" is not necessarily the greatest expert on time as experienced by finite humans.

I remember my early plane trips to Europe in the middle 1940s. The eastward trip in those days took sixteen hours and the return trip some twenty hours. One hopped from New York to St. John's in Newfoundland, from there to Shannon in Ireland, thence to Prestwick in Scotland, and from there to London and the Continent. At each of these stops the passengers had to leave the plane and were fed on the ground while the plane was refueled. I want to relate one experience because it illustrates the relativity of time and space. We had left New York at 5:00 P.M. and arrived in St. John's at 10:00 P.M. While we were herded into a dining room for a late dinner I saw another room all set to receive guests. I asked the stewardess whether I could have dinner there, whereupon she said with a horrified expression, "Oh, no. That's where we serve breakfast to the passengers coming from Europe." For them it was 4:00 in the morning.

I happened to be in Holland for a few days sometime in the mid-1970s when Mr. X, a member of the Dutch cabinet, vanished. He did not appear in his office, he did not attend the cabinet meeting, he did not come home. He was gone, just gone.

Mr. X's disappearance made the headlines all over Europe because it happened at the height of a controversy about NATO's choice of a new generation of fighter planes. Was it going to be General Dynamics' F-16 or France's Mirage? The Dutch vote was crucial and Mr. X was the great expert in the matter. It was on the eve of the final vote that Mr. X disappeared. In the early morning hours the police found him in some shabby joint. Later in the day the decisive cabinet vote was taken — I was told — on Mr. X's prestige. But, I asked naively, hadn't his prestige suffered from the previous day's and night's happenings, which were only the latest in a sequence of similar occurrences?

I was told that this was not so because during the war he had been imprisoned in a Japanese camp, and didn't I know that for some mysterious reason at that time, about thirty years later, the former inmates of Japanese and German concentration camps had begun to behave in strange ways? That the mental hospitals were full of people who after having lived normal lives for some thirty years suddenly awakened, screaming in the middle of the night out of their nightmares; that long-forgotten agonies were suddenly remembered; that their souls felt as if their bodies had been tortured but yesterday?

The same thing seemed to be happening to former camp inmates all over Europe. The approximate period of thirty years seemed but as yesterday when it is passed. So much for time's non-linear, yea, non-chronological, character. Is it possible that in the mid-1970s, when Mr. X disappeared, we were closer to the 1940s than the 1960s?

Recently I asked a retired neighbor how he was spending his

days. That, he said, was a problem he had not yet resolved. "Time weighs heavily on my hands." He had held a high executive position in a large corporation. I could imagine how he had spent his days working, first to get to the top and then to maintain himself there, with no time for anything but work. "I have no time," he must have said on a thousand occasions. And now time was weighing heavily on his hands.

In *As You Like It*, Shakespeare writes, "Time travels in divers paces with divers persons. I'll tell you who Time ambles withal, who Time trots withal, who Time gallops withal, and who he stands still withal."

For my neighbor, time stands still. With me, it gallops. That does not make me a better person, only a more compulsive one. In my remaining years I would like to learn to amble with time, leaving spaces for the enjoyment of beauty, both worldly and spiritual. It is hard to live that way in our competitive society.

Are there *any* institutions that offer a balanced relationship with time, a relationship that combines dedication to work with an ability to withdraw from it? This is not a rhetorical question. It is a practical question, and I think it has an answer. Some monasteries offer that way of relating to time. Ruth and I spent a brief retreat a few years ago with the Russian Orthodox Franciscans of New Skete in the mountains of upstate New York. There time had such a quality, balanced between manual work and worship. No monk would ever say, "Time weighs heavily on my hands," or, "I have no time." Each monk arranged his time in keeping with the alternating rhythms of his life.

Already, as a boy of five or six, I realized that there are two ways in which we experience the passing of time. After summer comes fall, then winter and spring, and summer again, a purely chronological experience. But I believed there was an alternative: to experience summer after summer after summer, autumn after autumn after autumn, winter after winter, spring after spring, parallel lines replacing a single undulating line. And the same would apply to one's birthday, or New Year's Eve, or Christmas.

One day when I was eighteen years old, I saw in a small theater in Vienna Thornton Wilder's play *The Long Christmas Dinner*. It is based on this very principle of parallel experience. The play is set in a family dining room where the table is spread for Christmas dinner. It covers a span of ninety years, from the 1830s to the First World War. The actors, as time progresses, put on wigs of white hair, and when their time comes they get up from their chairs and disappear through the open door hung with black velvet at the right of the stage. They eat imaginary food with imaginary forks and knives. Newborn children in their baby carriages are wheeled in through an entrance at the far left trimmed with garlands of food and flowers. In one of the many poignant scenes a new baby is wheeled in, the parents admire it as young parents will, but the nurse holds them off and pushes the carriage on through the door at the right.

The story is that of the Bayard family, who settled on the bank of the Mississippi River in Minnesota. They were the first family in a town that grew up around them. Toward the end of the play—in 1920 or thereabouts—the youngest generation rebels. One scene depicts the conflict between the father, Charles, and his son, Roderick, who had been drunk at the country club on Christmas Eve. When the father confronts the son they argue.

Roderick: Great God, you gotta get drunk in this town to forget how dull it is. Time passes so slowly here that it stands still, that's what's the trouble.

Charles: Well, young man, we can employ your time. You will leave the university and you will come into the Bayard Factory on January second.

Roderick: I have better things to do than to go into your old factory. I'm going somewhere where time passes, my God!

In the play ninety Christmas dinners are telescoped into one long Christmas dinner. As many summer sailing days could be telescoped into one long Summer Sail.

At my seventy-fifth birthday party, our children and grandchildren performed *The Long Christmas Dinner*. It was a moving experience because I felt as if the performers spoke their lines sometimes as members of the Bayard family and sometimes as members of our own family. The distinction was often blurred by the universality of Thornton Wilder's language.

Eight years have passed since then. Much has changed. Some who were in good health at the time are no longer with us. Some who were teenagers are married. Some who were married no longer are. Some who felt safe in their jobs have since lost them. There are new faces among us. Slow but relentless changes have taken place in our individual lives under the appearance of sameness. Some of these changes have caused great pain, others great joy. All mark the passage of time.

"Another year has gone," say the old. "Another year has come," say the young. These words seem to indicate that time passes faster for the old than for the young. Not even counting the very young. I remember that when I was in the lower grades of the Dutch elementary school, the six weeks' summer vacation which we mostly spent in the Austrian mountains lasted an eternity. Upon our return home I had to re-familiarize myself with the trusted environment from which I had become estranged during that long vacation, the beginning of which I had forgotten before the end was in sight. I realized that my parents did not have to go through this re-acquaintance process. To them six weeks were but as a watch in the night . . .

These words bring me back to the beginning of the chapter.

We have said some things about the relationship of time and space and about the differences in the subjective experience of time's passing. But it would take more to lift even a tip of the veil that covers time's enigmatic character.

II

HOPE

~9~

Hope

From classical Greek mythology Pandora comes to us, a woman of beauty and grace. When she is given in marriage to Prometheus's brother, Zeus provides as a dowry a box containing all the evils of the world and hope as well, with the understanding that she will not open it. But Pandora, driven by curiosity, does open it, and the evils escape before she can restore the lid. Only hope remains confined in the box.

Dr. Karl Menninger once noted that "the *Encyclopedia Britannica* devotes many columns to the topic of Love and many more to Faith. But Hope, poor little Hope. She is not even listed." Indeed sometimes it seems as if hope were still imprisoned in Pandora's box. Dr. Menninger's reference is to the famous passage from the thirteenth chapter of Paul's first letter to the Corinthians: "So faith, hope, love abide, these three; But the greatest of these is love." These words present one of the most eloquent statements on love in Western literature. They are popular reading material at weddings. I use them often and with great conviction.

But lately two reservations have weakened that conviction. First, no reason is given in the text *why* these three — faith, hope, and love — abide. The second reservation is more substantive: I am no longer convinced that the greatest of the three *is* love.

And if it is, I have begun to think that it should share that privileged position with hope. For our lives are based on hope; without it, life withers.

Hope and faith are related. Paul defines faith as "the assurance of things hoped for, the conviction of things not seen." If we have faith — says Paul — we *believe* our hopes will be fulfilled. Paul offers more than mere worldly optimism here.

Yet religious liberalism is an optimistic tradition, reflecting the mood of the eighteenth-century Enlightenment and of nineteenth-century rational humanism, with its quasi-creed of "onward and upward forever." But this mood could not do justice to, nor does it hold up under, the catastrophes of the twentieth century: the two world wars, the Holocaust, famine for hundreds of millions of human beings, the invention of means of total annihilation, the rising threats to our environment, the devastating epidemic of AIDS.

Blind optimism is not a realistic option, nor is it a spiritual one. Yet though our optimism fails us, religious liberals do not recognize pessimism as a valid option. The spiritual option is to find the line between optimism and pessimism that corresponds to the realities of life.

Pessimism and hopelessness are not the same. Pessimism has hope — though less hope than optimism, which is full of hope. The choice, then, is between more and less hope. Some degree of hope is always present. Without hope life has no purpose. Without hope, life cannot maintain itself. "For in this hope we were saved," wrote Paul to the young church in Rome.

> Now, hope that is seen is not hope. For who hopes for what he sees? But if we hope for what we do not see, we wait for it in patience.

Let me turn to Jean-Paul Sartre's play *No Exit,* one of the great literary illustrations of hopelessness. It is the story of the afterlives of three people, one man, Garcin, and two women, Inez and Estelle. Inez nurtures a lesbian love for Estelle. Estelle, in turn, lusts for Garcin. Garcin is in love with Inez. The emotional needs of each, therefore, are bound to remain unsatisfied.

The three find themselves in a room off an endless corridor that leads nowhere. The door is locked. There are no windows. The room is always lit. They never sleep. They are doomed to stay together forever. There is no hope. No hope at all, not even the hope for death, because they have already died. They are in hell.

Viktor Frankl, who survived four Nazi concentration camps, writes that the prisoner who lost faith in the future—that is, the prisoner who lost hope—was doomed: "With his loss of belief in the future, he also lost his spiritual hold; he let himself decline and became subject to mental and physical decay." Death would follow soon thereafter. One fellow inmate confided to Dr. Frankl that in a dream a strange voice had told him that the camp would be liberated on March 30, 1945. He had his dream in February. Dr. Frankl recalls,

> When [the prisoner] told me about his dream, he was still full of hope, but as the promised date drew nearer, the war news made it appear very unlikely that he would be free on the promised date. On March 29 he suddenly became ill and ran a high temperature. On March 30 . . . he became delirious and lost consciousness. On March 31st he was dead.

He was dead because his last hope had not come true. The prophecy was a false prophecy. Or was it? He certainly was liberated from his personal suffering on March 30, when he became delirious and lost consciousness. For him, the prophecy had come true.

In the early 1980s, the French philosopher/scientist François Jacob wrote,

It is hope that gives meaning to our lives. And that hope rests on the vision of being able, one day in the future, to transform the present world into a possible world which appears to be a better world.

And then he added,

When the novelist Tristan Bernard was arrested with his wife by the Gestapo, he said to her: "The time of fear is over. The time of hope has begun."

The time of hope supersedes optimism and pessimism and transforms fear. But hope must be more than a feeling; it must be related to doing. In Nazi-occupied Holland, hope became possible only when one acted and got others to act. Only then was fear transformed, only then did one experience hope.

~10~

Moments of Horror,
Moments of Hope

Ruth and I got engaged in February of 1939. Her parents approved of our engagement, but her father asked us to postpone our marriage until times were more normal. He was convinced—as were we—that war was imminent, and that the consequences for our native Holland would be disastrous, as they turned out to be. But I said to him, "If we wait until times are normal again, I will die an old bachelor and Ruth an old maid." He reluctantly accepted the answer. We were married in June. Three months later the war broke out. Ten months later the Nazis occupied Holland.

On the third day of the invasion, we tried to drive to Ymuiden on the Dutch North Sea coast. It was a vain attempt to get on one of the trawlers trying to cross over to England through the heavily mined waters of the North Sea in defiance of the German bombers and torpedo boats. Some people made it that way, others drowned or were picked up by German ships patrolling the coast.

Long before we got to Ymuiden we called the whole thing off. People—supposedly pursued by airborne troops—fleeing the coastal areas in the direction of Amsterdam, sniper fire, abandoned cars along the road, and columns of black smoke rising from burning villages, farms, and oil tanks at the horizon—all made us feel that the odds were against us. "Let's go home," Ruth said. "London will go up in flames. We will get out later." Which is exactly what happened.

Soon after the invasion the Germans instituted their racial laws. These applied to all "non-Aryans," that is, people who had at least two Jewish grandparents. We were among them. This meant complete disenfranchisement. Subsequently it meant deportation. Ultimately it meant death.

Of more than 120,000 "non-Aryans" in the Netherlands, fewer than 20,000 survived the Holocaust, and this number includes those who had gone into hiding and survived. We were among the persecuted, which meant that after a few months of occupation we were no longer allowed to travel, to go to restaurants, theaters, concert halls, parks, or other public places.

Ruth worked in those days in a day-care center for infants in a poor, predominantly Jewish part of Amsterdam. Some of the Jewish babies escaped the sinister end that awaited the majority because non-Jewish mothers — mostly inhabitants of the Jordaan, one of the poorest quarters of Amsterdam — took them into their homes: "I have so many children, the *Moffen* [contemptuous Dutch for Germans] won't notice whether there are a few more or less."

Early in the morning, when it was still dark, we would bicycle together to the day-care center, and from there I would proceed to the bank, though it was no longer allowed to employ me. An office, however, had been installed for me in the building next door so that I could continue to fulfill some of my duties. This arrangement had the advantage that the bank could keep an eye on me, for we had an understanding that if I had not turned up at a certain hour they would start a search. This precaution was taken not only because of the general danger, but also because Ruth's and my daily trips to the day-care center were not without risk. It is strange how once one is in danger, one gets accustomed to "living dangerously."

The U.S. Consulate in Rotterdam had been bombed out during the five-day war preceding the occupation. As soon as it reopened, we applied for immigration visas. This meant that I had to travel to Rotterdam, a risky but necessary undertaking. I do not know how many times I made that trip, but one day we traveled to Rotterdam together to receive the precious visa stamps in our passports.

Ruth, who had lived one year in Rotterdam, was upset when she saw for the first time the sight I had become accustomed to — square mile upon square mile of rubble where the city had been. By that time the streets had been cleared of debris, and it gave one a grotesque, surrealistic feeling to walk the well-known city streets while the houses on either side had disappeared. It is amazing how flat a city is once it has been reduced to rubble.

On the way back from the consulate we were hungry, and when we passed a small restaurant we decided to go in to get a sandwich and a cup of coffee, in spite of the fact that restaurants were off limits for us. I remember that while we were discussing whether or not to go in, I declared to Ruth — and the rubble — that after all, this was my country and to hell with the *Moffen*. So in we went.

While we were eating, several SS men came in and sat down at the table next to us. We did not leave before we finished our sandwiches and drank our coffee, partially out of pride and partially because a sudden departure might have aroused their suspicion. But the bread tasted stale and the coffee bitter.

Our life under German occupation oscillated between horror and normalcy, but it was clear that in the end the former would crowd out the latter. We synchronized our schedules: Ruth would come home from the day-care center after having fed the babies their main meal, some time early in the afternoon; I would await her telephone call from home and then leave the bank to join her. Thus we were "free" from the middle of the afternoon on—an unknown luxury. It gave me the opportunity to take my violin out of its case, which it had not left for many years, and start playing again. The combination of increasing food shortages and decreasing office hours gave us the idea to participate in a community garden. The thrill of the newness of this small venture preempted, at least for a few hours a day during those summer months, the feelings of anxiety and impending disaster. Our neighbors were generous with much-needed advice. We worked in wooden shoes, as they did, a technique that had to be learned at the price of many blisters.

We spent many hours there, happy ones I would say, though the dogfights that took place regularly overhead between German and British planes, some of which came down in flames, were so many reminders of the reasons that made me work in a community garden during banking hours.

In the winter months we went skating on the canal in front of the house. The air of festiveness that has always characterized the Dutch skating scene prevailed. But by the time we had reached our front door, skates in hand, it had been displaced by the more realistic feeling of despondency, if not despair.

At night we played rummy in our blacked-out bedroom. We kept a running score on the bedroom wall, and the lengthening columns of penciled figures made us marvel at the mystery of chance that made the difference between the scores in the end always oscillate around the zero point. Strangely, and in spite of the ominous conditions under which we lived, there were still moments of fun and happiness.

Outside the war raged. Schiphol was bombed at least once a week, and every night the antiaircraft batteries were in action against the British Flying Fortresses on their way to the Ruhr Valley. The German Green Police began their *razzias* (raids) first by day, but when these provoked strong protests on the part of the non-Jewish population, by night.

In the early months, when it was rumored that there would be *razzias* in our neighborhood, we slept a few times away from home. We found this so demoralizing that we decided to take the risk of staying at home, rather than uproot ourselves and, in the process, endanger our friends.

The apocalyptic atmosphere caused a resurgence of the belief in soothsaying and all kinds of future-revealing techniques. The word *belief* may be too strong. It was more that people in their desperation would try out anything that might reduce their suffocating apprehension with regard to even the most immediate future. I played my part in this revival of superstition, and one dark, wintry afternoon I visited a "highly recommended" old woman who lived on one of the canals and who, for a modest fee, would tell you the future.

She was reassuring: All was going to be well. Once out of the country, I was not going to get the job I expected to get, but another job would be waiting for me. Both predictions proved to be correct. Then the old woman said, "I see somebody around you who is very worried, very worried. Her name is Anna. Do you know somebody by the name of Anna?" I told her that I did. Anna was the name of my mother, who had died three years before.

Under the threat of annihilation, life gains in intensity. One of the main concerns we had in those days was to stay out of German hands because "once they get hold of you, you have had it." This did not prevent us from giving shelter to some German-Jewish youngsters the Nazis had chased from a farm north of Amsterdam, where they had been preparing for emigration to what was then still called Palestine. They slept for days in their sleeping bags on our living room floor and departed one day under the auspices of the Jewish Council.

I don't know what became of them, or rather, I am afraid I do know. I don't mention this incident as an example of great heroism on our part, because it wasn't, but it illustrates how under pressure from outside threats one does things one would not do under more normal conditions. When the threats grow beyond a certain point, life turns into death. I remember a mental picture I carried around with me in those days: under great pressure carbon turns into diamonds, but if the pressure grows beyond a certain point, the diamonds are pulverized.

That is what happened ultimately to the victims of the Nazi racial persecutions. That is the fate we were spared. The possibility for Ruth and me to comfort each other was never taken away from us. For reasons we don't know, it was given to us to escape the *danse macabre* that was performed by the inmates and the guards in the lunatic asylum of the Nazi world. We have never forgotten that but for the grace of God we would have been there until the gruesome end. Mixed into our gratitude — daily commemorated, though rarely mentioned — is a feeling of survivor's guilt: Why us and not the others? The real story is the story of those who did not get out.

Certainly we have known since those days that we live on borrowed time. So does everybody else, only we realized it at an early age, as do people who have been mortally ill early in life. Our mortal illness had been to witness the Nazi horror and the gruesomeness of its "final solution."

~11~

The Likelihood of the Unlikely

The book of Ecclesiastes is the one biblical book that denies the unexpected: "There is nothing new under the sun." These words depict a disenchanted world, a world in which the unlikely has been traded in for the obvious, the unexpected for the routine. But we live by dint of the unexpected. If the obvious would always prevail, if life were foreseeable, if everything would follow as the night the day, if there were no room for the discontinuous, the surprising, the miraculous, life would not be worth living. Thank God, that is not the way it is. As W. H. Auden described it, "the inevitable is what seems to happen to you purely by chance." Life is not lived by the rule but by the exception to the rule. We live by the likelihood of the unlikely.

Consider the life of Moses. He was an exception to the rule if ever there was one. According to Pharaoh's commandment "that every son that is born [to the Hebrews] ye shall cast into the river," Moses should have been drowned at birth. But the inevitable did not happen. Thanks to a most unexpected turn of events, he survived and was adopted by Pharaoh's daughter as her son. After he had grown up, Pharaoh learned of his existence and sought to kill him, but Moses fled to the land of Midian, out of Pharaoh's jurisdiction. There he married a daughter of the local priest. He was keeping his father-in-law's flock when the normal course of events was interrupted once again. God spoke out of a burning bush and charged Moses to prevail upon Pharaoh to let the children of Israel go.

Do I believe in the literal truth of this story? No. But I do believe that the story describes how things happen in this world. Not only Moses's life and the lives of other biblical giants but also our more modest lives develop from one unlikely, often seemingly miraculous event to another.

The moment when I set eyes for the first time on the woman who shortly thereafter would become my wife was such an event. It was at the wedding of a cousin of Ruth's that I attended together with a mutual friend. When I saw Ruth I asked the friend, "Who is that girl?" He said, "That is Ruth Melchior. Why do you ask?" I said, "Because I want to marry her. How old is she?" My friend looked bemused. "Seventeen or there-abouts," he said. "I'll wait two years," I said, unmindful of the possibility that she might meanwhile marry someone else, as she nearly did. When we announced our engagement after two years, an aunt of mine came to see me at my office. She told me that she had attended the wedding of Ruth's cousin together with my mother. My mother had pointed Ruth out to her, say-ing, "Who is that girl over there? She would be a good wife for Peter." My mother died a few months afterward. I felt as if she had posthumously blessed our union.

When we arrived in this country, the overriding problem that confronted us was the question that confronts most immigrants: how to make a living. I could have tried to find a job with one of the banks I had visited on my business trip to the United States in 1936, or at least asked them to assist me in finding a job. But somehow I didn't feel like doing that. In the end, we decided to buy a secondhand car and go west, where I was confident of making the $3,000 a year that we needed to live.

We bought an ancient Plymouth but postponed our depar-ture for a technical, financial reason. In the prewar years a number of Central European friends of mine had entrusted money to me. Though limited, these amounts of money represented their reserves — in some cases their only reserves — in case of need. Before leaving New York I wanted to obtain from the "enemy-property custodian" a license to pay out these amounts upon demand to the owners if and when they would reach non-enemy territory.

The negotiations with the enemy-property custodian took several weeks, and it was during those weeks that I received a telephone call from an old friend of my father's who was the managing director of a small bank in Amsterdam. He had just arrived in New York from the south of France, where he had taken refuge when the Nazis invaded the Netherlands. By sheer chance he had heard of our arrival and somehow obtained my telephone number. He wondered whether I was interested in assisting him in administering the assets of his bank. These assets, and in fact the bank itself, belonged to members of one of Europe's most distinguished banking families. My ensuing relationship with them determined the nature and scope of my banking career. The likelihood of the unlikely had prevailed.

The old Bible stories, as well as our own life stories, demonstrate the unexpected, the exception to the rule, the discontinuous, miraculous newness of it all. That is the stuff our lives are made of. Life thrives on the unexpected, the unlikely. Its rules are justified by the exceptions to the rules, its routines by the breaking of routine. Notions of chance or luck don't go deep enough to describe this phenomenon; they don't do justice to the mystery of life. Contrary to the proclamation of Ecclesiastes, there is nothing *old* under the sun.

~12~

Waiting

I don't know about you, but I find it exceedingly difficult to wait. Of course, there are many kinds of waiting. I can't say that I like any of them.

The other day I was to meet a friend at 4:00 P.M. at the corner of Beacon and Joy Streets in Boston. I am early, arriving at ten to four. I'll have to wait. Not pleasant, but okay. After all, it is I who am early. But when my friend is not there at ten *past* four, I begin to wonder will he ever come? Was there a misunderstanding? A car accident? And how much longer should I wait? Fifteen minutes? Half an hour? Meanwhile, cars are zipping by; people pass me. Their coming and going is purposeful. They know where and with whom they will be fifteen minutes from now, half an hour from now; I don't. In passing me, they are passing me by. Contemporary life passes me by. How long am I able to stand this? How long am I willing to stand this? I look around. Here he comes, muttering apologies and explanations. And I say, "It's perfectly all right." And in a way it is. My panic is gone; I am again a sensible part of a sensible scene. He was just twenty minutes late. What are twenty minutes? Big deal!

A young friend of mine described to me how he feels about the girl he is in love with. It is early in the afternoon and he is going to take her out for dinner. "But I can't wait five hours," he says. "I have to talk to her." "So why don't you call her?" I suggest. "Because if she's not in I'll feel rejected. And how will I get through the afternoon? What you don't understand is that I can't face life without her."

One day many years ago, Ruth was waiting for me in a car in the underground garage of a big bank building. I was attending a meeting on the umptieth floor, unable to extricate myself. Ruth went through agonies similar to those I described earlier, but she must have waited more patiently, more creatively, than I or my young friend, for she wrote this poem:

> Waiting is
> time suspended
> The clock's hands
> are stilled
> Sounds have lost
> all meaning
> Heartbeats count
> but hours do not
> It almost feels
> like falling snow.

In the book of Lamentations it is proclaimed that "the Lord is good unto them that wait for him," and the psalmist admonishes, "Rest in the Lord and wait patiently for him." But the destructive, the panicky, the hopeless side of waiting is also represented in our literary heritage. In T. S. Eliot's play *The Cocktail Party,* the Unidentified Guest, speaking to Edward, whose wife has just left him, says, "The one thing to do is to do nothing. Wait."

Edward: But waiting is the one thing impossible. Besides, don't you think that it makes me ridiculous?

Guest: It will do you no harm to find yourself ridiculous. Resign yourself to be the fool you are. That's the best advice that *I* can give you.

> Edward: But how can I wait, not knowing what I'm
>   waiting for?

An answer to that question appears in Samuel Beckett's play *Waiting for Godot*, the "song of songs" of the waiting fool. It is about two bums with the unlikely names of Vladimir and Estragon. In the play we witness two days—or years, or eternities, who knows?—of their life, together with its vicissitudes, its ups and downs, its frugal joys and black despairs—from Estragon's taking off his boots, which hurt, to an aborted joint suicide attempt, to their sad acceptance of their self-imposed task to wait for Godot. They do not know Godot. They wonder what he may *look* like, what he may *be* like. They do not know. They only know that they are waiting and that by his coming they will be saved.

Do we here find a trace of the Jewish messianic expectation? Could Godot stand for "God O.T.," God of the Old Testament? It just occurred to me. But I don't know. I do know that waiting, by itself, waiting without thinking much or doing anything, waiting not willingly or patiently or hopefully but just for the sake of waiting is not redemptive but destructive, while waiting willingly or patiently or hopefully can be the greatest of all blessings.

Vladimir and Estragon wait without hope, without patience. They live one step removed from suicide. They fill their days with empty talk and empty gestures, and while they tell each other that they are waiting for Godot, they are, in reality, not waiting at all. For waiting presupposes hope and patience—and stillness.

"Be still, and know that I am God," says the psalmist. Be still and know. Shut out the noise and the haste, the activity and the search, the motion that kills the emotion. In stillness we will come face to face with the great mystery into which we are born. And from that confrontation we will derive hope and patience and serenity.

"We do not obtain the most precious gifts by going in search of them but by waiting for them," says the mystic Simone Weil in her book *Waiting for God*. There is only waiting, attention, immobility.

We spend a major part of our lives waiting.

Waiting to be born and waiting to die.

Waiting to grow up and waiting to grow old.

Waiting for expectations to be fulfilled, for hopes to come true.

The quality of our lives depends on the spiritual mood in which we wait. For only when we wait empty of desire and preoccupation and busyness, will Truth come to us and will we be ready to receive it.

~13~

Having Fun

Fun derives from playfulness, the kind of playfulness that is the essence of our lives. The Dutch historian of culture Johan Huizinga wrote in his study *Homo Ludens* (Man at Play) that "play is older than culture."

> Animals play just like [people]. We only have to watch young dogs to see that all essentials of human play are present in their merry gambols. They invite each other to play by a certain ceremoniousness of attitude and gesture. They keep the rule that you shall not bite—or not bite hard—your [sibling's] ear. They pretend to get terribly angry. And—what is most important—in all these doings they plainly experience tremendous fun and enjoyment.

He concludes, "Nature . . . gave us play, with its tension, its mirth, and its fun."

Before the Second World War, people used to say, If you want the British to win a war, tell them it's a game; if you want the Germans to win a game, tell them it's a war. Today things are different. If you would tell either the Germans or the British that the game they are about to play is a war, the chances are that both would stop playing.

I'm not a tennis player, but I do enjoy the lean splendor of the annually recurring tennis tournaments at Wimbledon. And I remember, as some of you will, the bad manners indulged in by that great tennis player John McEnroe, a three-time winner at Wimbledon. The public resented his taking the fun, the playfulness, out of the game. For McEnroe did not, in the words of Huizinga, "pretend to get terribly angry"; he was in fact terribly angry, thereby destroying the playfulness and the fun.

Many years ago I participated in a number of meetings of representatives of two seminaries which were hardly on speaking terms though they belonged to the same denomination. Competition prevailed, and misunderstandings seemed destined to separate the schools forever. The purpose of the meetings was to explore the possibility of establishing a good working relationship between them. The first two meetings were not encouraging. Ghosts from the past poisoned the present. But I remember saying to Ruth after the third meeting, "I think we'll make it. Today we laughed together." Fun had entered our discussions. Life had prevailed over death.

Lately a number of books have dealt with the life-giving quality of laughter and playfulness. In one of these, *Head First*, Norman Cousins mentions an account written more than half a century ago, showing that hearty laughter stimulates internal organs, "making them work better through the increase of circulation." He wrote that laughter had the effect of brushing aside many worries and fears that otherwise set the stage for sickness.

Laughter is good physical exercise. But beyond that, it creates a mood that helps the forces of healing. It is not by chance that many hospitals engage clowns to entertain children who are patients, not only to break the monotony of the hospital day but, more important, to provoke the patients to laugh and thereby enhance their chances for recovery. Clowns bring fun into the sickroom. Fun and laughter are understood today to have life-giving powers.

When my mother was fifty-two years old she was diagnosed

as having cancer. In those days doctors were less inclined than they are today to give prognoses of the patient's life expectancy. One day she said to me, "At my age life is no longer fun." I knew then that she was dying.

During the lifetime of each and every one of us there are periods—they may be lengthy periods—when our lives are drained of fun. Periods of mourning, periods of grieving and despair. Then there is no room for fun. Life shrinks and deepens the perception of suffering.

Three years ago our oldest grandchild, Rachel, was diagnosed as having an inoperable brain tumor. When she experienced the shock of the diagnosis, when she suffered from the side effects of her radiation treatment, when we all cried a lot, she watched funny videotapes exclusively. Rachel wanted to laugh. Rachel wanted to live. Today she leads a full, rewarding, creative life, a life worthy of a gifted twenty-four-year-old. In spite of the continuing threat that hangs over her future, fun has reentered her life, as it has the lives of all of us, though, as our grandson Peter put it, "nothing will ever be the same again for any of us."

My friends, life is a serious matter, if only because—as far as we know—we live only once, and that one life is spent in the shadow of the knowledge that we will die. Within the framework of this seriousness it is the playfulness and the fun we have that give life its grace.

~14~

God or Whoever You Are . . .

His name is Robin Lee Graham. On July 27, 1965, when he was
sixteen years old, he set sail from San Pedro, California, on a
solo voyage around the world in a twenty-four-foot sloop
named *Dove*. It took him five years to complete the trip. Reli-
giously speaking, he was an agnostic. "Like many people of my
age," he wrote in his book *Dove*, "I had dismissed God and religion 'and all that stuff' as something packaged up with stained
glass windows, dreary organ music and an old man with a
beard." Off the coast of Madagascar, Robin ran into the worst
storm of the trip, a veritable hurricane. He was not sure that his
boat could take the beating.

> It is hard to remember what thoughts I had at the height of
> the storm. Some fear, yes, fear touching the edge of panic.
> But the instinct of survival depended on my keeping *Dove*'s
> stern to the sea and on keeping awake. . . . Brilliant flashes lit
> up the monster swells and filled the cabin with green light.
> Then the thunder roared above the noise of the sea. For the
> first time in my voyage I felt that *Dove* would not make an-
> other port. The seas were too big for her after all and I too
> tired to help her.
> My battery-powered tape recorder was soaked and the

reels wouldn't turn. So I turned the reels by hand to make one last recording. I said: I've just prayed to God, and I prayed long and hard to make the sea and wind calmer. I prayed, "God or whoever you are, please help me."

... I prayed with my arms locked round the tiller.

That was the moment when the storm began to abate. The huge swells stopped coming at me. I went to sleep. When the sun woke me up next morning, October 14, the wind was down to fifteen knots. The sea was sparkling and gentle.

Robin did not believe in God, the old man with a beard, but when push came to shove he turned to that very God, having nobody else to turn to.

God or whoever you are. What comes to mind is the old joke about Unitarian Universalists addressing their prayers "to whom it may concern." God or whoever you are. Robin addressed the source of all life and of all being. Still, his prayer was the prayer of an agnostic, literally, a "non-knower." As such, it raises the old question — to borrow from the theologian Martin Buber — of whether there is a "Thou" that the "I" encounters in a dialogue, a mutuality. Humanists do not think so, theists do. Existentialists do not think so, Jewish and Christian traditionalists do.

And then there are those who find themselves in a precariously balanced in-between position that Herman Hesse described when he wrote, "We become acquainted with that state of mind in which we are unable to decide whether the images on our retina are the result of impressions coming from without or from within." Hesse put these words in his hero's mouth: "We create gods and struggle with them, and they bless us."

Is this what Robin did when he prayed with his arms locked around the tiller, "God or whoever you are, please help me"? For that was the moment the storm began to abate. Don't ask me what would have happened if he had not prayed. Would the storm have gone on, would Robin have perished? All I can say is that he *did* pray. Does this mean that "God or whoever he is" does exist? Or did Robin, in Hesse's words, paraphrasing the story of Jacob and the angel, create God and struggle with God until God blessed, that is, saved him? I cannot answer the question, but I can say something about it.

In the Bible the human being is presented first as the creation of an all-powerful God who "formed man of the dust of the ground, and breathed into his nostrils the breath of life," but also as a being not wholly without influence on the nature of God — as one who influences, yes, at times, creates God. Let me give some examples.

In the eighteenth chapter of Genesis, Abraham bargains with God about the destruction of Sodom and Gomorrah. After winning his plea that God save Sodom for the sake of fifty righteous men, Abraham negotiates God down to ten righteous men. Even more important is Abraham's statement before the negotiation begins, when he

> stood yet before the Lord . . . drew near and said, "Wilt thou also destroy the righteous with the wicked? . . . That be far from thee to do . . . to slay the righteous with the wicked. . . . Shall not the Judge of all the earth do right?"

With these words Abraham takes the initiative. He reminds the Lord that he, the Judge of all the earth, shall do right. Indeed, who has made whom in whose image?

In the thirty-second chapter of Exodus, while Moses is speaking with God on Mount Sinai, the Israelites worship and bring sacrifices to the Golden Calf. God is furious: "I have seen this people, and behold, it is a stiff-necked people; now therefore let me alone, that my wrath may burn hot against them and I may consume them." Moses proves to be both more mature and more thoughtful than the Lord. He says,

O Lord, why does thy wrath burn hot against thy people,
whom thou hast brought forth out of the land of Egypt with
great power and with a mighty hand? Why should the Egyp-
tians say, 'With evil intent did he bring them forth, to slay
them in the mountains, and to consume them from the face of
the earth?' Turn from thy fierce wrath, and repent from this
evil against thy people." . . . And the Lord repented of the evil
which he thought to do to his people.

In the eleventh chapter of Numbers, the children of Israel
complained about their diet of manna and "wept . . . and said,
'Who shall give us [meat] to eat? We remember the fish, which
we did eat in Egypt freely; the cucumbers, and the melons, and
the leeks, and the onions, and the garlick. But now our soul is
dried away: there is nothing at all, beside this manna, before our
eyes.' " And now compare the Lord's reaction to that of Moses:
"The anger of the Lord was kindled greatly; Moses also was
displeased."

These biblical passages portray a certain superiority of
human beings to their God, as if they, the humans, were offering
an example to the deity. I have sometimes thought that we find
a trace of that in the Lord's Prayer: "Forgive us our trespasses
as we forgive those who trespass against us." It is as if we said,
Look what we are doing and follow our example.

Who created whom in whose image? I don't know the answer. All I can say is that I—and I know I am in good company—do pray as Robin prayed, trying to address myself to the
nameless, the unimaginable source of all life and of all being,
whoever or whatever it or he or she may be. That is what Robin
did when he prayed with his arms locked around the tiller. And
then the storm began to abate.

~15~

Fear of Darkness

*What price have we, as a people, paid for
this light? We have become afraid of the dark. . . .
Our souls shrivel up. For growth
of the human person takes place in the dark.*
MATTHEW FOX

*The dark [is] all that we are afraid of, all that we don't
want to see—fear, anger . . . grief, death, the unknown.*
STARHAWK

*Every study shows that fear of darkness is . . . common at
every age.*
JOHN BOWLBY

"The light shineth in the darkness; and the darkness comprehended it not." These words from the first chapter of John's Gospel are mysterious words. They could be construed to imply that light and darkness belong together but are somehow estranged; the darkness does not comprehend the light.

I remember as a three-year-old child lying in bed in the dark hours of the early evening. The world was full of frightening noises. Their mysterious nature was explained to me in terms which were equally mysterious, but the explanation of one mystery by another is somehow reassuring, as any theologian and many scientists know. Thus the loud and alarming sound of a bell, I was told, was "the fire engine"; the more varied tones of a trumpet, "the boy scouts coming home." What was a fire engine, I wondered, and what were boy scouts? In due time I would find out.

Then there was the chant of the flower merchant, pushing his cart through the street. (What was a flower merchant, I wondered, and what was a cart?) His voice rose up from the street like a ritualistic incantation and sounded something like this:

Ro - zen stam-ro - zen   le-lie-tjes-van daal
(Roses, hollyhocks   lilies of the valley)

It was followed by an ominous sounding cry: *"Ramenas! Ramenas!"* (*Ramenas* are black radishes.)

Freud tells the story of a three-year-old boy who calls out from his dark room, "Auntie, speak to me! I'm frightened because it's so dark." His aunt answers, "What good would that do? You can't see me." "That doesn't matter," replies the child. "If anyone speaks, it gets light." "Thus," comments Freud, "what [the boy] was afraid of was not the dark, but the absence of someone he loved."

"If anyone speaks, it gets light." Freud may be right, but I am reminded of the first chapter of Genesis: "God said, 'Let there be light'; and there was light." In both stories, one who loves speaks light into existence and thereby overcomes the darkness—the darkness of the boy's room, the darkness that was upon the face of the deep. It is significant that in the creation myth the creation of light precedes the creation of everything else. As if in that primordial darkness nothing could endure the utter fear of that darkness. Is our own fear of darkness an echo of that fear?

Light and darkness belong together, but, as the Gospel of

John implies, each somehow became estranged from the other. Could it be that light and darkness belong together because we need light in order to endure the dark? And we need the dark in order to grow?

We do need the dark. Human growth takes place in the dark, just like the deep, dark growth of a tree's roots. Indeed, life without darkness is no longer life, it is hell. Darkness, in turn, is unbearable without light. Maybe that is why they are estranged from each other. Perhaps light and darkness can be reconciled in the human being. There is, I believe, an example of such reconciliation in the closing lines of Dylan Thomas's *A Child's Christmas in Wales:*

> Looking through my bedroom window, out into the moon-light and the unending smoke-colored snow, I could see the lights in the windows of all the other houses on our hill and hear the music rising from them up the long, steadily falling night. I turned the gas down, I got into bed. I said some words to the close and holy darkness, and then I slept.

The boy's words were words of reconciliation.

Star Island is a rocky island ten miles from Portsmouth, New Hampshire. During the summer months it is used as a conference center. Life on Star Island is simple and infinitely engaging. The day begins and ends with a worship service in the chapel built a century ago by fishermen on the island's highest spot. In the evening, after sundown, in keeping with an old custom, the people mount the rocky road single file and in complete silence. Each person carries a lantern into the chapel and hangs it on the wooden brackets that extend from the white walls of the little sanctuary. As the silent chapel fills up the light gets stronger. The more people, the more light. The proceedings have always struck me as an ancient liturgy. Something is being acted out. Is it, possibly, a kind of reconciliatory celebration between light and darkness, a reflection of the harmony rooted in the knowledge that each owes its existence to the other?

For if it is true that darkness is both the feeding ground of our souls and also that which reminds us of all we fear, and if it is true that light can shrivel our souls and at the same time enlighten us and free us from our fear of the dark, then the estrangement of light and darkness can be resolved only when we free ourselves both from the fear of darkness and from the fear of light.

~16~

Living Every Moment

What is it that so often prevents us from listening to life's messages of meaning? I think it is our everyday worries—unpaid bills, unfinished tasks, physical discomforts, fatigue, troubled relationships with partners, spouses, and children, with colleagues, bosses, or subordinates, fear of the future, regrets of the past. And we say to life, You have to wait, I have no time now. First let me take care of all the trouble I'm in, and then I'll listen to you. What we forget or do not realize is that all the trouble we are in *is* part of life, and that in dealing with all that trouble we are living, as we should be living, every moment.

Living every moment makes sense only because our earthly life is not forever. From the moment of birth our days are counted, our lives are finite. In the psalmist's words,

> The days of our years are threescore years and ten; and if by reason of strength they be fourscore years, yet is their strength labor and sorrow; for it is soon cut off and we fly away.

The psalm concludes, "So teach us to number our days that we may apply our hearts unto wisdom." Count your days. But also let every day count.

The young, even if they know it intellectually, do not experience the finiteness of their lives emotionally. Their lives seem to stretch endlessly before them, beyond the horizon. But the older we are, the more frequent are the moments we live consciously. For with age comes an awareness that we do not live forever, that one day death will confront us. Contemplation of death makes us live more deeply. Tacitus, the Roman historian and poet, wrote,

> Death whispers in my ear:
> Live! I'm coming!

Death, the life-giver.

I said that the young do not experience emotionally the finiteness of life. As a rule this is true. But there are exceptions: the young who go to war and come back, or those who recover from a mortal illness, or those who face death. Many years ago the six-year-old son of a friend of ours, while riding his bicycle on the sidewalk, was hit by a car that jumped the curb. In the ambulance on the way to the hospital he said to his father, "I am going to die and I'm not afraid. Don't you be afraid." When the ambulance arrived at the hospital he was dead.

When Ruth's brother was told many years ago that he had a life expectancy of less than two years, he said to his sister, "We all have time-tickets tied to us, but contrary to most, I now know what is written on mine."

Some years ago our granddaughter Rachel, then twelve years old, spent time at Children's Hospital in Boston. Her roommate was a radiant seventeen-year-old high school senior who suffered from cystic fibrosis. One day Ruth found herself alone with Rachel's roommate, who sat crosslegged on the bed. She was excited about having met, earlier that day, a thirty-one-year-old executive who also suffered from cystic fibrosis. "When I was born," she said, "children born with cystic fibrosis

In the shadow of death my mother and I have We cannot solve the mystery of life and death.

had a life expectancy of one to five years, with few exceptions, and this woman is thirty-one years old. I don't know how long I am going to live, but I intend to make every moment count."

Those who have had an encounter with death derive from it a heightened sense of life. I had such an encounter not long ago. I had a ten o'clock appointment at the dentist's. One hour before the appointment I was to take four tablets of penicillin, which I did without knowing that I am allergic to the stuff. I found out when sitting in the dentist's chair. I was close to fainting, my lips and my tongue were swollen so that I could hardly speak. My blood pressure went down to 80 over 40.

In the ambulance on the way to the hospital I received injections of adrenalin and antihistamines; oxygen was also administered, and I hovered on the threshhold between waking and sleeping. I wanted to sleep but I was afraid I might not wake up again. I clung to the small margin of consciousness and I thought, "So this is what it feels like, this is the way it begins."

Three hours later I left the hospital healthy, hungry, and tired. I don't know whether, medically speaking, I had been close to death. Emotionally I had been. And I was warned that I would probably not survive a repeat performance.

In a way I am grateful for my experience in the ambulance. I have been reminded of things one likes to forget, I have learned from it not only with my mind, but with my heart. For I have rubbed shoulders—not for the first time, which would be unlikely at age eighty-four, but once again—with the great mystery of life and death that envelops us all.

Some of the moments I lived most intensely were the moments preceding the death of my mother. At age fifty-two she was hospitalized with terminal cancer. Many people said it was sad that she had to die so young. I remember thinking, "It *is* sad when parents die, but young? No." To their children parents are never young. At the time I was twenty-seven, the youngest vice president of a medium-sized Amsterdam bank, in charge of the foreign department. The job entailed a lot of travel abroad, which I kept to a minimum during my mother's illness. This enabled me to have lunch with her at the hospital almost every day. The luncheons were a source of comfort for both of us.

One day the president of the bank asked for me. He told me that a large American firm of metal traders had approached us for assistance. They wanted our bank to take charge of the daily finances of their London correspondent, and he asked whether I would be interested in going to London for two or three months to take charge of the operation.

I felt tempted to accept. But what about my mother's condition and our daily luncheons? That night I slept badly. When morning came I had reached the conclusion that the conflict was not simply between my ambition and my mother's need of me, because she was as ambitious for me, her only son, as I was. I decided to share the problem with her and ask for her opinion.

That day at lunch I told her the story. She listened attentively. When I was through, she asked, "Is it good for your career?" "Yes," I said. "Then you should accept," she said. And I did, but with the understanding that I would come home every Friday afternoon and stay in Amsterdam until Monday morning so that I could be with her during the weekend.

Over the next few weeks the new arrangement became routine. From day to day it had not been noticeable that she was losing ground, but from one weekend to the next it was quite evident. Then one Friday night a colleague was waiting for me at the airport. I was to go straight to the hospital, where the doctor was waiting for me. "If you had been here today we would have let her go," he said. "But she wanted to see you so badly that we kept her alive. You can see her now." I did, and we talked. I was with her when she died in the early hours of the morning.

In the shadow of death my mother and I lived every moment. We cannot solve the mystery of life and death, but we can say some things about it: that life derives its meaning from death, that life's nostalgic beauty stems from its finiteness, that life's meaningfulness can be experienced only in small doses, day by day, moment by moment. For it is not true that one day is like the other, one moment like the other. The deepest meaning of life can be fathomed only if we are aware of the uniqueness of each day and of each moment.

~17~

Living with Loss

Some losses cause such pain that it seems impossible to live with them. And still we do. Most of us have suffered and carry through life the burden of painful loss, often involving the death of a loved one. For loss is an aspect of death, though it is more broadly based. Losses stem not only from the discontinuity of life, but also from the discontinuities within life.

The words "my wife died" point to a loss stemming from the discontinuity *of* life. The words "my wife left me" point to a loss stemming from the discontinuities *within* life. So do the words "I lost my job," "our dog ran away," "we had to take father to a nursing home." Some of these losses may be recoverable. The loss caused by death is final. It leaves no hope. It has to be lived with.

I was told of an older man's feelings of utter desolation when, after a twenty-year relationship, his younger lover announced one morning that he was leaving him for another man. For several years the older man held out hope for his lover's return. The younger man died of AIDS and the older man's hope died with him.

When William Sloane Coffin preached a sermon about the death of his beloved twenty-four-year-old son, Alexander, he said, "When parents die, as did my mother recently, they take with them a large portion of the past. But when children die, they take away the future as well. That is what makes the valley of the shadow of death seem so incredibly dark and unending."

After our firstborn, a son named Jan Melchior, died unexpectedly of a vitamin K deficiency five days after his birth, in Amsterdam, on April 4, 1940, our mourning was aborted a month later by the Nazi invasion of Holland. The "phony war" had ended, the real war had begun, and the death of our little boy seemed to dissolve itself in the great calamity that was to bring death to tens of millions of people of all ages. Now, fifty-three years later, I have been wondering whether things would have been different if our grieving could have run its course. As it is, this son of ours has remained a presence in our lives and also—though to a lesser degree—in the lives of his younger sisters.

In his brief life our son gave us great happiness. If we could live our lives over again and were given the choice between having and losing him—the way it happened—or not having him at all, I know we would choose to have him. Has our memory of him, our recollection of the short days of his life, grown dimmer with the passage of time? I don't think so, because the past lives in us. It moves closer to our consciousness and recedes again like the tide. The past lives in us and the present is but the past's cutting edge. Maybe the cutting edge is as sharp as the past is alive.

Jan Melchior's coming and leaving us are not remembered as past events but are woven into the living fabric of our lives. That is why we don't whisper about him, but speak in a clear voice, as we speak about our other children, or about the bay and the garden. Jan Melchior's death was very hurtful, but the memory is not. It is part of that past that lives in us, but the nature of that past changes over the years. It evolves. A trans-substantiation takes place, and the factual realities of the past seem to become spiritualized, lifted out of their chronological context. Like everybody else we have our haunting memories. Like everybody else we have our non-spiritualized memories—conscious or subconscious—and our private nightmares. Jan Melchior's short life is not one of them. The days he spent with us were blessed days, and when we think of our children we think of him as one of them.

I was with him when he died in the early morning hours. Ruth was still confined to bed. That night I dreamed that a figure whose face I never saw entered his room wearing a black cloak and took him in its folds. Ruth has told me that she had a similar dream that same night.

There is a Dutch saying that shared joy is double joy and shared sorrow half sorrow. I used to believe that the second part of the saying was wrong, that shared sorrow was double sorrow because to one's own sorrow was added that of the other. Today I understand that the second part of the saying teaches us something about how to live with loss: by sharing it with others who have suffered a similar loss, we comfort them by making them realize that they are not alone in their sorrow, and derive comfort ourselves from that same realization.

~18~

The Business of Living

Between the mysteries of birth and death lies the business of living. There are changing phases in the human life cycle, each with its own special problems.

When our now middle-aged children were small, we lived according to the gospel of Dr. Spock. He taught young parents of our generation how to understand the child's evolution in six phases from birth to young adulthood. Erik Erikson distinguished eight stages of the completed life cycle. Joseph Campbell spoke of three stages: the dependency of childhood, the independence of maturity, and "the crisis of dismissal, disengagement, and, ultimately, death."

Sometime during maturity, possibly when we are in our late forties or early fifties, something happens to us that seriously affects our outlook. From my personal experience I would describe it as a turning from the cradle to the grave, which is shorthand for beginning to relate our daily life experience no longer to where we come from, but to where we are going.

From 1946 until my retirement in 1974, I headed an investment banking firm in New York City. Every year during the Christmas season, all employees from the president to the junior messenger boy sat down to a Christmas luncheon that had developed its own ritual. There were announcements of promotions and individual achievements; skits were produced that poked good-natured fun at colleagues and superiors; there always was a lot of laughter.

Anticipating my second career, I had already, in those days, developed the ministerial weakness of not being able to let a captive audience go to waste, so I would hold forth on these occasions, thanking people, praising people, encouraging people, and reminding them of the religious nature of the season.

These annual events were very dear to me, as they were to others. I was aware of the number of past Christmas luncheons, at least in the early years. But then I lost track of the number until I realized one day that—assuming my retirement at age sixty-five—the number of past Christmas luncheons I had attended exceeded the number of future ones I would attend. I began to count the remaining luncheons as I had counted the early ones, only now in reverse order: not how many I had attended—one, two, three, etc.—but how many there were left for me to attend—five, four, three, two, one. Thank you, Mr. Fleck, and goodbye!

This turnaround from cradle to grave is not the only change in perception that comes with age. The horizon of one's life shrinks in many ways, including geographically. During my banking years I would cross the ocean at the drop of a hat. Today the idea of crossing the Cape Cod Canal gives me a feeling of anxiety. But now I enjoy more deeply than ever before all the wonderful things on this side of the canal: my family, my ministry, the incredible beauty of the sun rising over Nauset and setting over the bay at Rock Harbor, the reflection of the full moon on Pleasant Bay.

It makes me think of the story of the old gentleman from the town of Eastham on the Cape, who was born there nearly seventy-five years ago. He spent his entire life in Eastham. He served the community in public and private ways; there was no position of trust in Eastham he had not filled at some time or other during his lifetime. When his seventy-fifth birthday approached, a committee was formed to plan an appropriate celebration. It was decided to offer him a trip to Europe, where he had never been. The old gentleman was very touched by the townspeople's kind intention, but he would not accept the gift. True, he said, he had never been to Europe, but he had not seen and enjoyed all of Eastham yet.

Last summer I sailed a lot. It was not because I had an excess of free time, because I had not. Rather it was because of my feeling that time is running out. I don't know how much longer I will be able to go sailing, and I love Pleasant Bay and Little Pleasant Bay and the islands and the Outer Beach and Broad Creek. I have always loved sailing, but in an odd way, the realization that it will not go on forever makes every sail a gift for which I am grateful.

Twenty years ago I might have liked to sail, say, in the Caribbean; today I have no such ambition. The horizon shrinks. But what life loses in expanse it gains in intensity and depth. I have mentioned the midlife preoccupation with commitments taken and fulfilled. After that comes the time to give up commitments, to disengage oneself from obligations, to free oneself from duties, to limit one's responsibilities.

Joseph Campbell's words come again to mind: "After you have gained your world comes the threshold of yielding it — the crisis of dismissal, disengagement, and, ultimately, death." We may be forced into that crisis by physical or mental infirmities, or maybe just because so much of our mental capacity and our interest is absorbed by that "living towards the end," by learning to give up control, by permitting ourselves to *be* controlled by the cosmic undulations of life and death, receiving and giving up, holding on and letting go.

It is in this spirit that we should greet every new day as the gift it is, full of things unknown and untouched, full of promise, full of hope.

III

LOVE

~19~

Come as You Are

At the far end of the Cape, in Provincetown, stands one of the most beautiful church buildings on Cape Cod. It is the Universalist Meeting House, built in Greek Revival style in 1851. Near the street is a sign announcing next Sunday's sermon title. At the top of the sign are the words "Come as you are." They have been there for many years. Their meaning is clear: You do not have to dress up to be admitted to the service, you are welcome as you are.

It has occurred to me that the words "come as you are" can be given a deeper meaning, a cosmic meaning: We do not live in a judging universe in which we may ultimately be weighed and found wanting, but in an accepting universe, a universe that welcomes us as we are, that embraces us with open arms, the "everlasting" arms mentioned in the book of Deuteronomy.

This is good Universalist theology. In the end, nobody is found wanting; God will not condemn any human being to eternal suffering in hell. The Unitarians have come to a similar conclusion by a slightly different rationale. It has been said facetiously that Universalists believe that God is too good to damn humans to hellfire, whereas Unitarians believe that humans are too good to be damned. Both represent an ultimately optimistic world view in which the only exhortation is the one Polonius gave to his son Laertes in *Hamlet:* "To thine own self be true."

In a book of Jewish wisdom, I found, a long time ago, the story of Rabbi Zusya. Before he died, so the story goes, Rabbi Zusya said to his flock, "In the world to come they will not ask me, 'Why were you not more like Moses?' They will ask me, 'Why were you not more like Zusya?' "

If we come as we are, does that mean that we can please ourselves and do whatever suits us at that moment, avoiding the difficult, the painful, the unappealing, the self-sacrificial? No. The invitation to come as you are is subject to one condition, spelled out in Paul's letter to the Philippians: "Do nothing from selfishness or conceit, but in humility count others better than yourselves. Let each of you look not only to his own interests, but also to the interests of others." Be yourself, short of hurting others. And if there is no way to avoid hurting others, then at least hurt them as little as possible.

To come as we are and to be who we are also demands courage, the kind of courage that enabled Luther to post his ninety-five theses on the door of the Wittenberg Cathedral and to exclaim, "Here I stand; I can do no other." "This," he seemed to say, "is what God intended me to do."

If we are to come as we are, there must be those who receive us as we are. On the cosmic level, the universe embraces us as we are. On the human level, we depend on others to welcome us as we are. And those who welcome us will in turn be welcomed by others.

The Dutch, who have a knack for saying things well in an unpoetic way, tell us, "Dare to be who you are." "Come as you are" is really an invitation to take the dare. It is an admonition to act in keeping with our own being, our own nature. It is a summons to not be ashamed and to live up to the intentions God has for us.

Those among us who cannot muster the courage to be who they are risk losing their identity, but if you can learn to accept the liberating invitation to "come as you are," you may risk finding it.

~20~

Humility

And what does the Lord require of
you but to do justice, and to love kindness,
and to walk humbly with your God?
MICAH 6:8

Unlike most prophetic admonitions, Micah's does not spell
out an ethic but a way of life. It does not deal with theology but rather with applied religion. It does not speak to the
question What do you believe? but to the question What do
you do?

The surprise lies in the admonition "to walk humbly with
your God." *Your* God, as if to confirm that every human being
has the privilege of holding a personal concept of the Divine. A
truly liberal religious insight, an insight that says something
about the nature of humility.

If I make money into a god, or my honorary degrees, or my
chauffeured Cadillac, I make things into gods. But these gods
are idols and their veneration is idolatry. The God who inspires
humility is the God of the great mystery into which we are born
and of which we are a part, the God of creation, the God of
whom the psalmist says, "He has made us and not we ourselves;
we are the sheep of his pasture," the God who, in the fifty-fifth
chapter of Isaiah, declares,

> For my thoughts are not your thoughts, neither are your ways
> my ways. . . . For as the heavens are higher than the earth, so
> are my ways higher than your ways and my thoughts than
> your thoughts.

This is a beautifully poetic way of saying, I am that mystery and you will never understand it. But, says Micah, that is all right. We are not supposed to understand. There are only three things the Lord requires of us: "to do justice, to love kindness, and to walk humbly with [our] God."

These are religious requirements. They do not explain the mystery; they are derived from it, as is all religion. Indeed, religion could be defined as the insights that derive from the great mystery without explaining it in any way. And it is not by chance that these first two requirements pertain to our relationship with others, for it is in our relationship with others that we express our religion. Religion happens among people.

It is not always easy to be humble. A Dominican monk described to a lay person the fields of activity in which the various monastic orders specialize. "Take the Trappists," he explained. "They derive spiritual insights from observing silence. The Jesuits, of course, are the intellectuals and teachers among the orders, the Franciscans feed the hungry, clothe the naked, and take care of animals. We Dominicans meditate a great deal on humility. I think I may say that in humility we are tops."

Early in my preaching career I learned some tough lessons about humility. I remember one Sunday morning when I was to preach in the local Y for a newly organized fellowship. The congregation consisted of a handful of people, maybe ten or twelve. I felt well prepared. I had given the sermon once before and it had been well received. It could not miss.

Well, it did. It was as if the small congregation and I did not occupy the same space. My voice did not reach them, nor did my soul. I learned that morning that you cannot preach out of self-assurance, but only out of humility.

The word humility comes from the root *hum,* which we find in the Latin word *homo* and its English equivalent *human.* From the same root comes the Latin word *humus,* which means "soil" or "dust." Our very name, *homo* —human—should remind us at all times of the words attributed in Genesis to the Creator, who, after forming man of the dust of the ground and breathing into his nostrils the breath of life, said, "You are dust, and to dust you shall return."

In the great creation myth, we humans are made of the dust, the humus, the earth. Our dust-ness, our humus-ness, our humanity and humility, are built into us. They are activated by our constant awareness of the mystery when we walk with the God who *is* that mystery.

Our knowledge of the universe has increased since the days of Micah, when people believed that the earth was the pancake-shaped center of the universe. What treasures science has revealed since those days, what insights it has produced! And still that mystery remains; it does not yield to our knowledge.

When I grew up there was a widespread belief among unchurched people that one day in the foreseeable future science would replace religion. That belief has dwindled. Today it looks as if science and religion move on different levels, as if they will never collide or replace each other but will coexist and be harmonized in the human being who may be made from the lowly humus of the ground but who is inspired by the breath of God.

We are inspired by forces outside ourselves. Many preachers know this, as do many performing artists. The cellist Gregor Piatigorsky once said to me, "Of course it is I who sit there and play the cello. But the inspiration, the genius, that which moves us, comes from the outside and expresses itself through me." If we ever forget that things are not done *by* us but *through* us, we will be in trouble.

Saint Francis prayed, "Lord, make me an instrument of Your peace." The prayerful desire to serve as God's instrument is an expression of the ultimate humility.

~21~

Giving and Receiving

In the third chapter of John's Gospel we read,

> For God so loved the world that he gave his only Son, that whoever believes in him should not perish but have eternal life.

These words present the essence of orthodox Christian beliefs. Theologically I cannot accept them, but emotionally they are very dear to me. I am moved by them and feel that all the gifts we make to those we love are echoes of that great mythical gift God gave to the world. Making gifts to those we love is a religious act, a holy thing.

In the book of Acts, the apostle Paul admonishes the faithful to remember "the words of . . . Jesus, how he said, 'It is more blessed to give than to receive.' " Actually, Jesus never said such a thing, at least no such utterance has been recorded in the Bible. In Matthew's Gospel—as in Mark's—a woman comes to Jesus while he is having a meal at the house of Simon the leper. She pours a precious ointment on his head. The disciples are indignant, saying, "Why this waste? For this ointment might have been sold for a large sum and given to the poor." If Jesus had agreed with them, if he, too, had reprimanded the giver, she would have been left embarrassed, feeling guilty, humiliated. But he said to his disciples, "Why do you trouble the woman? For she has done a beautiful thing to me. For you always have the poor with you, but you will not always have me." He made the gift a blessing to the giver by receiving it gratefully.

Meanwhile, the idea that giving is somehow superior to receiving survives. Erich Fromm wrote in his book *The Art of Loving*, "Giving is more joyous than receiving," and also that "love is primarily giving, not receiving." Still, he admitted that "in truly giving, [one] cannot help receiving that which is given back."

In a love relationship, people experience the joy of giving themselves to each other and receiving each other. In a love relationship giving and receiving become one. In only one respect does giving differ from receiving. The process of giving and receiving can begin only with giving; we speak of "giving and receiving," not of "receiving and giving." In the beginning is the gift.

When, in the words of Genesis, "God formed man of dust from the ground," God "breathed into his nostrils the breath of life." God gave the gift of life to the human being he had created. No gift, not even God's gift of life, is possible without a receiver. It is equally true that in order to receive there must be a giver. And the way in which the receiver receives the gift determines whether that gift will be a blessing or a curse.

The purest gift I can imagine is a handful of flowers picked by a child and offered with outstretched hands. The way in which the adult receiver receives the gift may determine whether that child will grow up as a generous or as a reluctant giver. "My, look at the beautiful flowers. Are they really for me? Will you help me put them in water?" or, "Don't you know that you should not pick flowers from my garden? And look at the mess you made on the floor!"

The joy of giving stems from the joy with which the gift is

received. The child who is reprimanded for having picked flowers out of "my" garden is embarrassed and feels guilty.

In a loving relationship, gifts are constantly given and constantly received, by touch, by eye contact, by the exchange of words and gestures, in a million different ways. The intensity of that exchange is a measure of the intensity of the love that exists between the lovers. When that exchange suffers and diminishes, the relationship withers.

In Jean Paul Sartre's play *No Exit*, a conversation occurs between a man, Garcin, and a woman, Inez:

Inez:	What were you saying? Something about helping me, wasn't it?
Garcin:	Yes. . . .
Inez:	And what do you expect me to do in return?
Garcin:	To help *me*. It only needs a little effort. Inez; just a spark of human feeling. . . .
Inez:	It's no use. I'm all dried up. *I can't give and I can't receive.* [Italics mine.]

The conversation takes place in hell.

In the early days of our marriage, Ruth and I knew an old Jewish couple who had escaped from Nazi-occupied Vienna to Amsterdam. For years they had not spoken to each other. They lived together in a silence of hatred. There was no communication between them, no giving, no receiving. They had created a hell on earth. Two years after we met, their private hell on earth was merged into the public hell of Hitler's gas ovens, in which they perished, I suppose without exchanging a word.

A colleague once told me about the many parishioners who came to her for counseling. "When they leave they thank me for giving them advice. But I always feel that I ought to thank them for giving me their confidence." Giving and receiving are inter-twined.

Five hundred years ago, Saint Francis of Assisi wrote, "For it is in giving that we receive." As it is in receiving that we give. That is the law of love. That is the law of life.

~22~

Love and Respect

One of the Beatitudes reads, "Blessed are the peacemakers, for they shall be called children of God." What strikes me is the implied assumption that conflicts among people will always exist, that enmity is an inevitable component of life, yes, even of love. The emphasis in the Sermon on the Mount is not on the avoidance of conflict but on reconciliation:

> If you are offering your gift at the altar, and there remember that your brother [or sister] has something against you, leave your gift there before the altar and go; first to be reconciled to your brother [or sister], and then come and offer your gift.

If you would say to me, "My husband (wife) and I are very happily married. Neither of us ever raises his (her) voice. Neither of us ever slams a door. Neither of us ever offends the other," I would be inclined to think either you have a very poor memory or you are lying through your teeth. For in this life conflict is inevitable, even among those who love each other, even among the most peace-loving people. It is wonderful to be obliging and turn the other cheek. But how many cheeks does one have? One soon runs out of cheeks. And then the yelling starts. Or the swallowing. I don't know what is worse, to express one's anger or to swallow it, to give ulcers or to get them. Personally, I have always been more inclined to express my anger. I'm not proud of it, and whenever I do it, it makes me feel guilty. Over the years I have gained the insight that in order to get rid of my sense of guilt I must overcome my anger, reconcile, and make up.

Paul, in his letter to the Ephesians, specifically allows us to be angry, that is, as long as we make up before the day is over: "Be angry but do not sin; do not let the sun go down on your anger." It is all right to be angry, but it is not right —indeed, it is sinful— to let the sun go down on our anger. We must overcome our anger; we must make peace without delay.

Peacemaking presupposes the presence of two essential elements, respect and love. By respect I mean one's recognition of the other person's dignity. One person's respect is the other person's dignity. If I disrespect a person I deny that person's dignity. Disrespect evolves into contempt and to treating the other person as a subhuman being to whom the restraints ordinarily observed among humans do not apply.

All genocide begins with disrespect. The Holocaust began long before the victims were fed into the ovens, by excluding them from the human community, by denying them their dignity as human beings, by making them into nonpersons, yes, anti-persons, parasites, a threat to humankind.

A similar condition preceded the genocide of the Native Americans. Indians were vilified as "no good"; "The only good Indian is a dead Indian," General Sheridan is supposed to have said. The abomination of slavery, too, was based on the thesis that blacks were not human. Slavery rested on the master's denial of the slave's humanity. Slaves had no dignity; they were owed no respect.

No democratic society can exist without mutual respect among its members —*all* its members. That is why those who denied that slaves were subhuman *had* to go to war to make them free, thereby saving the Republic, which indeed could not exist "half slave and half free."

The word *respect* does not appear in the Bible. The Bible does not speak of democracies but of hierarchies, of kings and subjects, of masters and slaves, of priests and congregations, of prophets and the people, of leaders and the led. It speaks of theocracies and aristocracies, not of democracies. The recognition of respect as distinct from love, the concept of respect by itself, may have been a rather late Western invention. And then again, the love Jesus preached did imply respect, based as it was on the commandment to love our neighbor as ourselves, which makes our neighbor a participant in our self-respect.

In Greek there are five words for love: love as friendship *(philia)*, love as affection *(storge)*, romantic love *(eros)*, sexual love *(karnos)*, and the greatest of all, *agape,* selfless, unconditional love, the love I feel not because I like somebody or because I am related to somebody or feel attracted to somebody, but because that other person is part of God's creation, yes, because in looking into that other person's face I come as close as I ever will in this life to looking at God. And I adore God in that other person. I looked up the meaning of *adore* in the dictionary and was delighted to find that it means "to regard with the utmost love and respect." Love and respect.

Agapate allelous! Love one another with *agape,* we are admonished in John's Gospel. Respect one another, I translate freely. Love one another with loving respect and respectful love, realizing that this is the only relationship worthy of our shared humanity.

~23~

Loving the Stranger

Why did God destroy Sodom? I mean, why specifically? It is not spelled out in the Bible. The reason God gives to Abraham is a very general one: "because the outcry against Sodom and Gomorrah is great and their sin is very grave." The nature of that very grave sin is not mentioned.

You might ask, Why, for heaven's sake, should we here at Cape Cod, or in New York or St. Paul, or wherever we are, be concerned in our day and age about the reason the God of the Old Testament decided more than four thousand years ago to destroy two villages at the southern end of the Dead Sea? What does that have to do with us? Well, it has a great deal to do with many of us. For this story has been used by millions in this country, in our time, to justify their homophobic condemnation of the gay lifestyle. They believe that in this story God condemns homosexuality as a very grave sin. "For isn't it clear," they say, "that the men of Sodom demand that Lot deliver the two visitors to them for what the *Jerome Biblical Commentary* describes as 'unnatural purposes,' " adding, between parentheses, "whence the modern term *sodomy*"? That is why the story of Sodom and Gomorrah is of great importance to us. It is this story on which many fundamentalists base their obscene theory that AIDS is God's punishment for homosexuality.

What, then, *was* Sodom's sin? In my opinion it was not homophilia at all, but xenophobia. It was Sodom's hatred of foreigners and the most excessive form of inhospitality, the mistreatment of strangers, revealed at the height of the controversy between Lot and the men of Sodom: "And they [the men of Sodom] said, 'This fellow [Lot] came to sojourn, and he would play the judge! Now we will deal worse with you than with them,' " referring to the fact that Lot was not a native of Sodom but one who came to live there as an adult. Sodom's "very grave sin" was its lack of hospitality, and not its alleged sexual preference. Strong support for this interpretation can be found in the use Jesus makes of this story. When Jesus sends out the twelve disciples to "the lost sheep of the house of Israel," he stipulates,

> If anyone will not receive you or listen to your words, shake
> off the dust from your feet as you leave that house or town.
> Truly, I say to you, it shall be more tolerable on the day of
> judgment for the land of Sodom and Gomorrah than for that
> town.

To Jesus, the Sodom story was apparently the utmost in inhospitality. That, in his opinion, was its sin. It had nothing to do with sexual preference.

As John J. McNeill observes in his book *The Church and the Homosexual*, the Sodom story includes the first of many biblical admonitions to love, to shelter, to protect, to feed the stranger: "Love ye therefore the stranger: for ye were strangers in the land of Egypt" (Deut. 10:19).

Why is the Bible so preoccupied with the stranger's fate? There is, of course, a practical aspect. The ancient world had no hotels or motels, no bed-and-breakfasts, no YMCA or YWCA, just a few inns along the routes of the most important caravans. Travel, whether for business, diplomatic, political, or personal reasons, depended largely on the willingness of private persons to take in strangers and to protect them against threats. In order to induce them to do so, the love of strangers was presented as an important religious duty and the lack of that love as a grave sin.

There may have been a deeper reason. For isn't it true that in a way we all are strangers? Aren't we all part of that mystery, that incredible, inconceivable, yes, scandalous mystery that leaves us ignorant of the meaning of birth and death, of the whence and the whither, suspended between unknowns and unknowables, strangers in a strange land? A. E. Housman's words come to mind:

> I, a stranger and afraid
> In a world I never made.

The psalmist wrote:

> Open thou my eyes that I may behold
> Wondrous things out of thy law.
> I am a stranger in the earth:
> hide not thy commandments from me.

Having lost their paradisical home, Adam and Eve became strangers in this earth. Noah embarked on his voyage leaving behind the familiar and the known. Abraham left the land of Ur and became a stranger in the land of Canaan. In the book of Deuteronomy, Moses commands his descendants to "make response before the Lord your God, a wandering Aramaean was my father," as if to wander as a stranger on the face of the earth was the mark of holiness. Lot was a stranger in Sodom. Joseph was a stranger in Egypt. Jesus was born on the road, in the stable of an inn. His life was that of a traveling teacher. During the short time of his ministry he went from one place to another, a stranger everywhere. He described his own fate when he said,

"The foxes have holes and the birds of the air have nests; but the Son of man hath nowhere to lay his head."

The Son of man was a stranger. And he identified with strangers everywhere. "I was a stranger, and you took me in."

In 1918, a cousin of Ruth's, then eight years old, fled Russia with her parents and siblings to escape from the Communists. Her titled father was a partner in the leading private banking firm in the country, and the family was known for its philanthropic activities, which made them a prime target of Communist persecution.

The journey took many weeks, and they faced considerable hazards. The one crucial moment (in every flight there is the crucial moment, the miraculous, the incredible saving grace) came when they had reached the border of White Russia, which was closed to refugees. An elderly, semiliterate peasant who functioned as a border guard and perfunctorily inspected their identity papers suddenly looked up and said, "I know that name; I shall never forget it. Your father once gave a pair of shoes to my father." And he let them through.

All of us are strangers. That is the one thing we have in common, the one thing we all share. That is the reason the admonition to love the stranger is repeated again and again in the Bible, throughout the Old and the New Testaments, from Genesis through Paul's epistles. The commandment to love strangers means that we are to love the stranger *in each other*. But if we love the stranger *in* each other, we are no longer strangers *to* each other. The love of the stranger overcomes the stranger's strangeness.

~24~

The Outsider

We may not be able to define what makes a person an outsider, but we recognize an outsider when we see one.

I was not born in this country. I did not go to school here; I am not emotionally involved with the Red Sox or the Yankees or any other team, and I speak the English language with a foreign accent — "as if you had just come off the boat," our children used to say an eternity ago, when they were teenagers. The perfect outsider, you may say, and I would agree. But not long ago I attended a retreat for Unitarian Universalist ministers. And there, among my colleagues, I was an insider. So we can be insiders in one context and outsiders in another. All of us, at times, have felt like outsiders, and many have disliked that experience. Don't despair; take heart. I hope to convince you of the worthiness of being an outsider.

The dictionary defines *outsider* as a person who does not belong to a particular group or party. It offers some examples: "Society often regards the artist as an outsider," and "Not being a parent, I was regarded as an outsider." According to this definition, one can be an outsider on racial, cultural, or ethnic grounds, or as a result of professional activities (an artist) or sexual preference (gay men and lesbians). We do not have to be clairvoyant to understand why the great feminist author Audre

Lorde, who was black and lesbian and a single mother of two children, called her book of essays and speeches *Sister Outsider.*

The outsider, as a member of a minority, is in many ways a handicapped person. On the other hand, perhaps because they have a different outlook on the insider's world, outsiders can perceive problems from an unusual perspective and discover solutions to which the insider is blind. This may account for the high number of instances in which decisive leadership—for good or for evil—has been exercised by outsiders. Napoleon was a Corsican, not a Frenchman, and spoke French with a Corsican accent. Hitler was an Austrian, not a German. Stalin was a Georgian, not a Russian. All spoke with the accents of their birth. William the Silent, the Dutch "Father of the Fatherland," was born in a German state and raised at the Spanish- and French-speaking Court of Charles V in Brussels. He did not speak Dutch at all. When he was murdered by a Spanish agent in 1584, he spoke his last words—familiar to every Dutch school child—in French: *"Mon Dieu, ayez pitié de moi et de mon pauvre peuple"* (My God, have mercy on me and on my poor people).

There are biblical examples of outsiders, too. Moses was adopted and raised as an Egyptian prince by Pharaoh's daughter, and he became the greatest leader in the history of the Jews. We don't know whether Moses spoke Hebrew with an Egyptian accent; he probably did. Jesus was a Galilean, an outsider in Jerusalem, where people reacted to the name of his native town with the question "Can anything good come out of Nazareth?" In addition, Jesus may have spoken the local Aramaic with a Galilean accent, for when Peter denies his Lord after his betrayal in the Garden of Gethsemane, a woman in the crowd says, "This fellow was also with Jesus of Nazareth." And they that stood around said to Peter, "Surely you also are one of them; for your speech betrays you." Peter spoke with a Galilean accent. Questions of language and accent have been and continue to be of vital importance in human relations and in who is the outsider.

When I grew older I learned how to live simultaneously in a number of different worlds, to each of which I belonged only in part, without losing my identity. All of us do this to a degree. It enriches our lives as long as it does not fragment our personalities. You have to be one and the same person in the different worlds in which you move. If you can do that, it can be a blessing to be the outsider. It may be painful, but it can also be tremendously creative, as worldly and biblical history show, to play the outsider's role in society, providing new perspectives, new initiatives, new solutions.

Don't relinquish being the outsider. We may be the outsider only sometimes, but we should love and respect the outsider at all times.

~25~

Making Our Peace with the Past

I wish I could leave history alone. Or rather, I wish that history would leave me alone. I mean my personal history. The things that have happened to me and the things that have not happened to me. The things I have done and the things I have left undone. I wish I could make my peace with these things. But I can't. Sometimes I lie awake at night, wishing I had done what I have not done, wishing I had left undone what I have done. And I realize that I missed opportunities for happiness because I didn't know that they existed; had I known, I would have seized them. I realize that I often neglected to experience life at any given moment, by itself and for itself and not as a stepping stone to something else.

This is not to say that I have not known happiness. I have known great happiness. But I have, too often, not savored that happiness at the moment when it occurred. Too often I have experienced my happiness only looking backward—"I realize now that at that time I was happy"—or by looking forward—"In anticipation of this or that I am happy." Or in any other form of what you might call "circumstantial happiness," rather than savoring happiness when it occurred consciously, knowingly, unconditionally, existentially, without implications and consequences.

I have often failed myself. I have stood in the way of my own happiness; at times I have been my greatest enemy. I find it hard to acknowledge that. But the past bothers us, and we carry its conflicts with us.

Still, what is the good of my fighting yesterday's battles against myself or against those who failed me? For I was not my only enemy. There was an army of them, which at times included my parents. They nurtured me, they loved me, they protected me — or at least tried to do so — at times. But how often did they, and the legion of teachers and relatives and parental friends and siblings (I had nearly forgotten the siblings), close doors that had better remained open, open doors that had better remained closed, ask questions that had better remained unasked, have no time when I badly needed their time. Their intentions may have been of the best; my parents were good people. There was not a cruel bone in their bodies. And still I have sleepless nights, or at least sleepless hours, trying to figure it out, trying to make things fit, trying to reinterpret past events in an effort to make them more acceptable, to get rid of some of the embarrassment, some of the feelings of inadequacy and failure they instilled in me, as well as feelings of guilt I can only get rid of by forgiving myself. I am thinking of relationships that turned from intimacy into enmity because I failed to see that the other person's actions that I resented resulted from that other person's pain and suffering.

It is as if I have spent my life making pieces of a huge puzzle. How amazing — and how gratifying — that the pieces fit together and that in the still-unfinished puzzle I can discern the pattern of my life. But in trying to complete the puzzle, I find that certain pieces are missing and others seem to have no place. And it is late in the day. I have no time to create the missing pieces, no time to restructure the puzzle in order to create room for the spare pieces. The whole thing doesn't add up. At least not with a high degree of perfection, which, in my book, would mean that all the pieces fit together, leaving no holes and no extras.

But God does not seem to share my idea of perfection. And I begin to think that maybe there are meant to be holes and spare pieces, holes through which God's breath can flow, spare pieces that suggest alternative arrangements of the puzzle. So these days I say to myself, What fits, fits; what does not fit is meant to stimulate me to greater creativity.

From this point on, any further preoccupation with my past is a waste of time. The memories of negative experiences that shamed or embarrassed me are there, as they are in the lives of each and every one of us, unalterably, immutably. There is nothing any one of us can do about them but accept them, live with them, and ultimately cherish them. Yes, cherish them. For lately I have come to believe that these negative experiences may well be what life is all about, that success is not the absence of failure, but the overcoming of failure. Not the absence of weakness, but the overcoming of weakness. Not the absence of mistakes, but the acceptance of mistakes, which means the forgiving of the mistakes. For we have the right to make mistakes; we are supposed to make mistakes. Things seem to be structured that way.

If we were to be castigated, banished, thrown into outer darkness for having made mistakes, life would add up to a practical joke, and I do not believe it is. We will make our peace with the past when we learn to forgive ourselves for what we have done and left undone, and then learn to live with both.

~26~

Honoring Your Father and Your Mother

Thinking about the past makes me think about my parents. Many people have lost one or both parents. They may feel that what I have been thinking about does not apply to them, but they are wrong. Well before we lose our parents to death we have internalized them, so our dialogue with them continues after death has parted us. For isn't it true that all of us are still engaged in this dialogue with our parents?

The Bible says something of fundamental importance about our relationship with our parents in the fourth commandment, Honor your father and your mother.

The word *honor* has always troubled me here. The commandment does not say that we should love our parents, or feel grateful to them. It doesn't say that we should follow their example. It says that we should honor them, that is, that we should hold them in high respect, regardless. That can be very difficult. Maybe before we can honor and respect our parents, we have to forgive them. It is here that a question arises, because one or both parents may have dealt with us in ways that are unforgivable. Think of the disastrous statistics according to which one out of three to four girls, and one out of six to ten boys, is sexually abused before the age of eighteen, often by a member of the immediate family, sometimes by a parent or by someone else with the knowledge and passive agreement of a parent, or as a result of the negligence of a parent. One begins to wonder whether we have a right to assume that all acts committed by parents are forgivable.

I do not have a good record in forgiving my parents. It is my father I have trouble with. He was a spoiled child, the youngest of five. He grew up to be an undisciplined man, given to unreasonable outbursts of anger that forced me at an early age into a reversal of the child-parent role. To my surprise, I still find myself resenting the fact that I was never given the chance to act out as a child or as a teenager. My father died at age fifty-nine, when I was twenty-one years old. His death ended an unhappy marriage that had lasted for nearly twenty-five years and had brought little joy to either him or my mother. He wanted to receive and give warmth but he had not learned how to do either. His kindness was clumsy, his emotionalism childish. But there was no malice in him, and he would have been incapable of doing anything mean. That is why I am not proud of my inability to forgive my father.

The sadness of my parents' marriage has taught me that feelings of love are of no avail if there is no knowledge of the ways to express these feelings in a manner acceptable to the loved one. There is a vocabulary of love consisting not only of words but also of gestures and attitudes, of touch, symbols, and style, that has to be learned in order to be known. Apart from loving our children we cannot give them a better preparation for life than to teach them that vocabulary. Meanwhile, my unforgiving attitude toward my father has put me on the track of an answer to the question of how to deal with the unforgivable.

I have found it helpful to distinguish between the act and the person committing the act. The fact that an act may be unforgivable does not necessarily mean that the perpetrator cannot be forgiven. We need to take certain facts into consideration. First, the perpetrator also had parents, or other people who raised him

or her. Second, in committing acts that hurt others, the perpetrator may have been driven by a misguided need for love.
Third, in the end perpetrator and victim share a common humanity that sometimes can become the basis of forgiveness.

For this to become possible, we must first learn to forgive
ourselves. It is a variation of the commandment to love our
neighbor as ourselves: to *forgive* our neighbor as we forgive ourselves. We forgive ourselves by accepting the fact that as human
beings we are fallible, that we are bound to make mistakes. If we
experience our mistakes in this way, we will create a basis for
forgiving ourselves that can become the basis for forgiving others.

If I want to forgive my father, I'd better get going, for time is
running out. I'm getting old. I nearly wrote that I've suddenly
gotten old. Which is, of course, nonsense, because time flows
evenly. Or does it? We don't experience time flowing evenly,
but in quantum jumps. Things appear quiet and steady. Whatever change takes place is imperceptible. And then, suddenly—
BINGO—overnight, so to say, we have grown older.

I've just experienced such a quantum jump. And it has reminded me of my unsettled account with my father. I don't remember ever having had a serious conversation with him about
any subject of general or personal importance. The intimacy,
the interest in each other's opinions, the mutual trust needed for
such a conversation just didn't exist between us. But from
where I stand today, I realize that he may have missed that
intimacy and that interest and that trust as much as I did. He
may have said, "It's too bad I cannot get through to that boy.
Whenever I want to talk with him he is evasive and just doesn't
respond."

Besides, I do not exclude the possibility that my mother may
have been not only the victim of her bad marriage but also its
coauthor. But that is not for me to judge. I am not supposed to
judge, but to honor my father and mother. My mother has not

made it difficult for me to honor her. As far as my father is concerned, I have come closer than ever before to honoring him. In my efforts to honor him I think I have come close to forgiving, yes, to loving him—somewhat. At least to the point that if we ever meet again—which possibility I do not exclude at all—I would say to him with real interest, "Hello, Papa. How are things with you?"

~27~

Prague Remembered

The First World War came to an end in November 1918. In 1920, my mother, her three brothers, and their families — eighteen people in all — spent the summer together in the Bohemian mountains. It was an ethnically diverse group. My mother, the youngest of four, had left her native Prague at a very early age to marry my father, who lived in Amsterdam. Her oldest brother married a French woman and lived with his family in Paris. Her two younger brothers and their families lived in Prague.

Being twelve years old I was allowed to travel to Prague and spend the weeks preceding our joint family vacation with my favorite uncle, my mother's youngest brother. His wife and their two children, the nursemaid, and the cook had already moved to their summer home. My uncle and I were the sole inhabitants of their Prague apartment. During the day he would be in his office and I would roam the cobblestone streets of the old city, with its smells of beer and smoked meat and holy water, its secret passages and alleys, its coffee houses and taverns. The baroque mysteries of *Zlata Praha*, the "Golden City," have never lost their fascination for me.

In the evening we would dine in some exotic restaurant (it was probably a normal Czech or Austrian restaurant, but to me it was exotic), and return home late enough to buy the next morning's newspaper. The dirty breakfast dishes piled up in the kitchen, the old newspapers in a corner of the bedroom — it was bliss, undiluted bliss.

I was also shown the sights — the thirteenth-century synagogue whose Rabbi Loew, in the sixteenth century, had created and subsequently destroyed the Golem, the prototype of the sorcerer's apprentice and granddaddy of our modern day robot; the street of tiny houses where the alchemists pursued their obscure prescientific magical efforts to transmute less noble metals into gold; and, higher up on the hill, the Hradchin, the glorious medieval castle of the kings of Bohemia, built around the Gothic Cathedral of St. Vitus. One afternoon when we walked in the Hradchin garden we met President Tomas Masaryk, who, unattended, was taking a breather and politely doffed his bowler hat in returning our greeting. Post–World War I Czechoslovakia was a real democracy.

Prague's Rabbi Loew took on even more significance for us only a few years ago, when a cousin of Ruth's sent her the following story, found among the papers of her father, who was born in St. Petersburg in 1863:

> Our ancestor Rabbi Jehuda Loew lived in Prague around the middle of the sixteenth century. His reddish tombstone can still be seen in the city's Jewish cemetery. He was an eminent scientist, and it is known that he corresponded with Tycho Brahe, the famous astronomer.
>
> The death of Jehuda Loew was the object of another legend. When he was very old, and having lost his wife, his daughter took care of him. He was at all times absorbed by his studies, and the only worldly interest he still had was the well-being of his child.
>
> When the time came for the Angel of Death to call the precious soul of the old man, he was unable to divert him from

his holy writings. As long as the learned man was engrossed in his studies of God, the Angel had no hold over him. He devised all kinds of tricks to draw his attention, but it was in vain; he was unable to divert the Talmudist from his books.

Thereupon the demon transformed himself into a rose. When the Rabbi's daughter went for a walk in the garden, she saw the beautiful flower, picked it, and brought it to her father. She opened the door to his study and cried: "Look, father, what a beautiful rose I picked for you; I just brought it in from the garden." When he heard his daughter's voice, the old man turned around with a smile on his face. At that moment, the Angel of Death took the opportunity to seize the soul of our ancestor, and he died in the arms of his daughter.

In 1938 the Nazis annexed Austria and occupied the Sudeten province of Czechoslovakia under the infamous Munich Pact that was supposed to buy "peace in our time." In the end it bought only one year of peace which enabled many of my Prague relatives to leave before the Nazis occupied their country.

After the war none of them were able to return to Prague, as that martyred city was "liberated" from the Nazis by the Communists.

~28~

Growing Up and Growing Old

I grew up in Amsterdam with Robert, my friend from kinder-garten days. In the late thirties, Robert was a member of the management of a Dutch trading company whose main business was in Central America. When war threatened to engulf Europe, he moved to Curaçao in order to manage the company's affairs outside of Europe in case the company was cut off from the Dutch management, which was exactly what happened. During the war years we saw each other frequently, as we did after the war, when Robert returned to Amsterdam. His business brought him regularly to New York; mine brought me regularly to Amsterdam.

When we both retired in 1974, his visits to the States continued. For Robert loves to travel; he will board a plane for any reason to any destination at the drop of a hat. When I was ordained in 1984, Robert flew over for the occasion. Whenever he stays with us over the weekend he comes to church to hear me preach. His last visit was memorable, at least for me, for on that occasion I realized for the first time the unique role Robert plays in my life. The fact of the matter is that he and I not only grew up together, we also grew old together. In my life there has been only one other person of whom this was true, my sister, and she died ten years ago. If I survive Robert there will be nobody left with whom I grew up and with whom I grew old. For those with whom I grew up and those with whom I grew old are different people. They belong to different cultures. They speak different languages.

I share this fate with most immigrants who came to the United States at a mature age. They all are growing old with people they did not grow up with. Those who grow very old may outlive all those they grew up with and, by outliving them, lose the witnesses of their youth. They have nobody to share memories with. Nobody to verify a story here, a happening there. And in the absence of witnesses, history becomes vague and unreal. Did it really happen? I would not be surprised if such persons, such survivors, having nobody left with whom they grew up, with whom they shared their early years, will feel that they have become, in the psalmist's words, "stranger[s] in the earth."

The loss of people one grew up with is not limited to immigrants or survivors. It may be the result of any estrangement from the environment into which one is born. It may also be the result of the mobility of our modern society. A hundred years ago, eighty percent of the population of this country lived on farms. Today four percent do. On the farm people usually died where they were born, with the people they grew up with. It was the America portrayed in Thornton Wilder's play *Our Town*.

Today most people do not live and die where they were born. They do not grow old with those they grew up with. In this sense most of us are "strangers in the earth." So — in his own words — was Jesus. Remember, when he was told that his mother and his brothers stood outside asking to speak to him, he said, " 'Who is my mother and who are my brothers?': And stretching out his hand toward his disciples, he said, 'Here are my mother and my brothers! For whoever does the will of my Father in heaven is my brother, and sister, and mother.' "

Take any congregation. How many members went to school together? How many share memories of their early years? Very few, I would guess. How many feel close to their biological families? I hope that many do, but I wouldn't be surprised if at least some of us, if we were told that our parents or our siblings were standing outside wanting to speak to us, would stretch out our hand to our congregation and say, "Here are my brothers and my sisters and my mother," testifying to the fact that the estrangement from those we grew up with has made us more susceptible to new relationships, built not on shared memories but on shared beliefs. Not on the past but on the present.

On his last visit I asked Robert many silly questions about unimportant matters: What, again, was the name of that French teacher whom we all loved and nevertheless teased mercilessly? What was the name of that place in the country where the juniors and seniors used to spend their fall and spring vacations? It was burned down during the war. And I realized that if Robert was unable to answer my questions I would have nobody else to turn to for an answer. It would be as if the whole thing had not happened. For the reality of the past depends on the presence of witnesses. We all need witnesses, and in their absence the past threatens to get lost.

This insight, that history needs witnessing, that without a witness there is no past and therefore no history, was the source of a cruel game the guards played on the inmates of the Nazi concentration camps. After a particularly hellish day the guards would say to the inmates, "None of this will ever be known outside of the camp. The knowledge of your suffering will die with you. There will be nobody to tell the world what happened to you. And if, by chance, some of you survive nobody will believe them." The prospect of oblivion, the threat of not becoming part of history, made the prisoners feel that their suffering was in vain, that they were being robbed of the last remnant of meaning that history might have given their fate.

History is the part of the past that has escaped oblivion, and in order to escape oblivion someone must testify. Without Plato,

Socrates, who never wrote a word down, might have fallen into oblivion. Without the Evangelists and the apostle Paul, Jesus could just as well not have lived, for the only time Jesus is mentioned in the Bible as having written something is when the scribes and the Pharisees brought the adulterous woman to him and asked him a tricky question about how to punish her. Then we read that "Jesus stooped down, and with his finger wrote on the ground." We will never know what it was he wrote in the sand of the Judean desert.

In the life of humanity as a whole, the witnesses are the artists, scientists, and historians of all times. In our own lives the witnesses are the people we grow up with and the people we grow old with. In my life there is only one surviving witness, Robert.

Inevitably, growing old means losing our witnesses, and, in a way, losing our life. When there is no longer anyone to check with about a forgotten name, no one to discuss distant events, it means that the past dissolves. But at least I have written these words about my witness, and perhaps in some small way they will outwit the passage of time. I know it will at best be for a short while only, beyond which looms the inscrutable mystery.

Index

119